Crime Victims with Developmental Disabilities

Report of a Workshop

AF896526

Committee on Law and Justice

Joan Petersilia, Joseph Foote, and Nancy A. Crowell, *Editors*

Commission on Behavioral and Social Sciences and Education

National Research Council

NATIONAL ACADEMY PRESS
Washington, DC

NATIONAL ACADEMY PRESS • 2101 Constitution Avenue, N.W. • Washington, D.C. 20418

NOTICE: The project that is the subject of this report was approved by the Governing Board of the National Research Council, whose members are drawn from the councils of the National Academy of Sciences, the National Academy of Engineering, and the Institute of Medicine. The members of the committee responsible for the report were chosen for their special competences and with regard for appropriate balance.

The study was supported by Contract/Grant No. 1999-IJ-CX-0031 between the National Academy of Sciences and the National Institute of Justice. Any opinions, findings, conclusions, or recommendations expressed in this publication are those of the author(s) and do not necessarily reflect the view of the organizations or agencies that provided support for this project.

Suggested citation: National Research Council (2001), *Crime Victims with Developmental Disabilities: Report of a Workshop.* Committee on Law and Justice. Joan Petersilia, Joseph Foote, and Nancy A. Crowell, editors. Commission on Behavioral and Social Sciences and Education. Washington, DC: National Academy Press.

International Standard Book Number 0-309-07318-9

Additional copies of this report are available from National Academy Press, 2101 Constitution Avenue, N.W., Washington, D.C. 20418

Call (800) 624-6242 or (202) 334-3313 (in the Washington metropolitan area)

This report is also available online at **http://www.nap.edu**

Printed in the United States of America

Copyright 2001 by the National Academy of Sciences. All rights reserved.

THE NATIONAL ACADEMIES

National Academy of Sciences
National Academy of Engineering
Institute of Medicine
National Research Council

The **National Academy of Sciences** is a private, nonprofit, self-perpetuating society of distinguished scholars engaged in scientific and engineering research, dedicated to the furtherance of science and technology and to their use for the general welfare. Upon the authority of the charter granted to it by the Congress in 1863, the Academy has a mandate that requires it to advise the federal government on scientific and technical matters. Dr. Bruce M. Alberts is president of the National Academy of Sciences.

The **National Academy of Engineering** was established in 1964, under the charter of the National Academy of Sciences, as a parallel organization of outstanding engineers. It is autonomous in its administration and in the selection of its members, sharing with the National Academy of Sciences the responsibility for advising the federal government. The National Academy of Engineering also sponsors engineering programs aimed at meeting national needs, encourages education and research, and recognizes the superior achievements of engineers. Dr. William A. Wulf is president of the National Academy of Engineering.

The **Institute of Medicine** was established in 1970 by the National Academy of Sciences to secure the services of eminent members of appropriate professions in the examination of policy matters pertaining to the health of the public. The Institute acts under the responsibility given to the National Academy of Sciences by its congressional charter to be an adviser to the federal government and, upon its own initiative, to identify issues of medical care, research, and education. Dr. Kenneth I. Shine is president of the Institute of Medicine.

The **National Research Council** was organized by the National Academy of Sciences in 1916 to associate the broad community of science and technology with the Academy's purposes of furthering knowledge and advising the federal government. Functioning in accordance with general policies determined by the Academy, the Council has become the principal operating agency of both the National Academy of Sciences and the National Academy of Engineering in providing services to the government, the public, and the scientific and engineering communities. The Council is administered jointly by both Academies and the Institute of Medicine. Dr. Bruce M. Alberts and Dr. William A. Wulf are chairman and vice chairman, respectively, of the National Research Council.

COMMITTEE ON LAW AND JUSTICE

Charles F. Wellford (*Chair*), Center for Applied Policy Studies and Department of Criminology and Criminal Justice, University of Maryland
Alfred Blumstein, H. John Heinz III School of Public Policy and Management, Carnegie Mellon University
Ruth Davis, The Pymatuning Group, Inc., Alexandria, Virginia
Jeffrey Fagan, School of Law, Columbia University Law School
Darnell Hawkins, Department of African American Studies, University of Illinois at Chicago
Philip Heymann, Center for Criminal Justice, Harvard Law School
Candace Kruttschnitt, Department of Sociology, University of Minnesota
Mark Lipsey, Department of Psychology and Human Development, Vanderbilt University
Colin Loftin, School of Criminal Justice, State University of New York at Albany
John Monahan, School of Law, University of Virginia
Daniel Nagin, H. John Heinz III School of Public Policy and Management, Carnegie Mellon University
Joan Petersilia, School of Social Ecology, University of California, Irvine
Peter Reuter, School of Public Affairs, University of Maryland
Wesley Skogan, Center for Urban Affairs, Northwestern University
Cathy Spatz Widom, Departments of Criminal Justice and Psychology, State University of New York at Albany
Kate Stith, School of Law, Yale University
Michael Tonry, School of Law, University of Minnesota

Nancy Crowell, *Study Director*
Karen Autrey, *Senior Project Assistant*

Preface

The Committee on Law and Justice (and its predecessor, the Committee on Research on Law Enforcement and Criminal Justice) has conducted work on criminal justice and related issues since 1975, when it was formed at the request of the administrator of the Law Enforcement Assistance Administration. The committee applies the knowledge and tools of the social and behavioral sciences to the development of improved policy, research, and evaluation related to criminal and civil laws and the operations of the justice system. It does so primarily by synthesizing, analyzing, and evaluating relevant scientific research related to critical issues in crime and justice at the federal, state, and local levels.

For fiscal year 1999, the committee was asked to conduct activities related to the criminal victimization of people with developmental disabilities. This activity arose under provisions of the Crime Victims with Disabilities Awareness Act (Public Law 105-301), which directed the attorney general of the United States to conduct "a study to increase knowledge and information about crimes against individuals with developmental disabilities that will be useful in developing new strategies to reduce the incidence of crimes against those individuals" (Section 4(a)). The statute authorized the attorney general to contract with the National Academy of Sciences to undertake this study.

The National Research Council (NRC) of the National Academies, in consultation with the National Institute of Justice, U.S. Department of Justice, determined that insufficient research on criminal victimization of people with disabilities existed to warrant a consensus panel study by the NRC. Instead, a workshop to discuss the state of the research and highlight gaps in knowledge was deemed the appropriate mechanism. The Committee on Law and Justice convened the Workshop on Crime Victims with Developmental Disabilities on October 28-29, 1999, in Irvine, California, at which authors of several commissioned papers delivered the results of their research. The workshop brought together policy officials from the Department of Justice, the Department of Health and Human Services, the Department of Education, the California Department of Developmental Services, and representatives from academia and the public sector. The latter included primarily criminologists, economists, law enforcement officials, policy analysts, psychologists, sociologists, members of the legal profession, and statisticians who have studied victimization of vulnerable populations, generally, and that of people with developmental disabilities, specifically.

Presentations and discussions focused on conceptual issues, including:

- Definitions and measurements;
- The ways in which theory on crime victimization can be applied to vulnerable victim populations;
- The existence of common themes or elements with regard to victimization experiences of vulnerable groups that would permit better measurement of rare or stigmatizing events that people are reluctant to report;
- The nature and adequacy of criminal justice and social service systems' response to vulnerable victims, especially those with developmental disabilities; and
- Whether research information from different sources within criminal justice system reports, surveys, and research studies on victims with disabilities and other vulnerable victim groups can be combined in ways better to inform the design of a new generation of studies on vulnerable victims.

In developing the workshop, the committee drew on information and expertise from other National Research Council work related to this topic, other research, and international, national, state, and local databases and reports.

The chapters in this report draw on the eight papers presented at the workshop. The report also draws on the oral presentations of paper authors and on comments made by a panel of distinguished commentators at the workshop. A list of the papers and authors appears in the Appendix.

The report draws attention to gaps in knowledge about the criminal victimization of people with disabilities. It is my hope that this report will stimulate research to begin to fill those gaps.

This report has been reviewed in draft form by individuals chosen for their diverse perspectives and technical expertise, in accordance with procedures approved by the Report Review Committee of the National Research Council (NRC). The purpose of this independent review is to provide candid and critical comments that will assist the institution in making the published report as sound as possible and to ensure that the report meets institutional standards for objectivity, evidence, and responsiveness to the study charge. The review comments and draft manuscript remain confidential to protect the integrity of the deliberative process.

We thank the following individuals for their participation in the review of this report: Linda Cottler, Department of Psychiatry, Washington University School of Medicine; William F. Eddy, Department of Statistics, Carnegie Mellon University; Susan Herman, National Center for Victims of Crime, Arlington, Virginia; Robert Scott, Center for Advanced Study in the Behavioral Sciences, Stanford, California; and James Short, Department of Criminology, Washington State University.

Although the reviewers listed above provided many constructive comments and suggestions, they were not asked to endorse the report nor did they see the final draft of the report before its release. The review of this report was overseen by Charles Wellford, Center for Applied Policy Studies, University of Maryland. Appointed by the Commission on Behavioral and Social Sciences and Education, he was responsible for making certain that an independent examination of this report was carried out in accordance with institutional procedures and that all review comments were carefully considered. Responsibility for the final content of this report rests entirely with the authoring committee and the institution.

Joan Petersilia
Workshop Chair

Contents

1

Introduction

Although violent crime in the United States has declined over the past five years, certain groups appear to remain at disproportionately high risk for violent victimization. In the United States, people with developmental disabilities—such as mental retardation, autism, cerebral palsy, epilepsy, and severe learning disabilities may be included in this group. While the scientific evidence is scanty, a handful of studies from the United States, Canada, Australia, and Great Britain consistently find high rates of violence and abuse affecting people with these kinds of disabilities.

A number of social and demographic trends are converging that may worsen the situation considerably over the next several years. The prevalence of developmental disabilities has increased in low-income populations, due to a number of factors, such as poor prenatal nutrition, lack of access to health care or better perinatal care for some fragile babies, and increases in child abuse and substance abuse during pregnancy. For example, a recent report of the California State Council on Developmental Disabilities found that during the past decade, while the state population increased by 20 percent, the number of persons with developmental disabilities in California increased by 52 percent and the population segment with mild mental retardation doubled (Frankland, 1996).

In addition, because of deinstitutionalization and new legislation, particularly the Personal Responsibility and Work Opportunity Reconciliation Act of 1996, many people with developmental disabilities now live in unsafe community settings where they get little health care, have access to few social services, and are easy targets for criminal predators. Fully a third (34 percent) of adults with disabilities live in households with a total income of $15,000 or less, compared with only 12 percent of those without disabilities (Harris, 1998).

WORKSHOP IMPETUS

Because of a growing concern among parents and advocates regarding possible high rates of crime victimization among persons with developmental disabilities, Congress, through the Crime Victims with Disabilities Awareness Act of 1998, requested that the National Research Council of the National Academy of Sciences:

> conduct a study to increase knowledge and information about crimes against individuals with developmental disabilities that will be useful in developing new strategies to reduce the incidence of crimes against those individuals. The study . . . shall address such issues as: (1) the nature and extent of crimes against individuals with developmental disabilities; (2) the risk factors associated with victimization of individuals with developmental disabilities; (3) the manner in which the justice system responds to crimes against individuals with disabilities; and (4) the means by which states may establish and maintain a centralized computer database on the incidence of crimes against individuals with disabilities within a state.

Because of the scarcity of empirical research on these issues, the National Research Council and the U.S. Department of Justice agreed that the best way to fulfill this mandate was to convene a workshop, rather than a full-scale study, to bring together researchers, practitioners, legal scholars, and advocates to discuss the state of knowledge in this area and highlight gaps in the research. This report provides details of important issues that were discussed at the workshop but, under National Research Council rules for workshop reports, does not draw definitive conclusions nor make recommendations.

For the purposes of this request, the legislation further defined developmental disabilities, in accordance with P.L. 42 § 6001(8), as follows:

> The term developmental disability means a severe, chronic disability of an individual 5 years of age or older that is attributable to a mental or physical impairment or combination of mental and physical impairments; is manifested before the individual attains age 22; is likely to continue indefinitely; results in substantial functional limitations in three or more of the following areas of major life activity—self-care; receptive and expressive language; learn-

> ing; mobility; self-direction; capacity for independent living; and economic self-sufficiency; and reflects the individual's need for a combination and sequence of special, interdisciplinary, or generic services, supports, or other assistance that is of lifelong or extended duration and is individually planned and coordinated, except that such term, when applied to infants and young children means individuals from birth to age 5, inclusive, who have substantial developmental delay or specific congenital or acquired conditions with a high probability of resulting in developmental disabilities if services are not provided.

As we discuss in this report, there are many different definitions of disability that have been used in research and data collection. However, these definitions do not necessarily coincide with the legal definition cited above.

A number of factors have impeded data collection and research efforts on the victimization experiences of vulnerable populations, including those with developmental disabilities. One involves reporting problems associated with vulnerable victims and stigmatizing events—for example, the reporting of sexual abuse of young children, elderly people, or people with disabilities who are dependent on caregivers. A second factor involves the problem of how to identify individuals with developmental disabilities and the behaviors against them that constitute crimes. A third is the apparent weakness of criminal justice system responses when cases that involve vulnerable victims are reported to the authorities. In general, there is a paucity of information about the characteristics of victims and offenders, as well as the interpersonal dynamics and contextual factors that may lead to abuse, neglect, and exploitation.

SCOPE OF THE REPORT

This report draws primarily on the papers and other presentations that were made at the October 1999 workshop. It addresses the following broad questions listed in the National Research Council's proposal:

- What is known about the nature and extent of crimes against vulnerable victims, including persons with developmental disabilities, and the risk factors associated with victimization, and what more do we need to know in order to reduce these crimes?
- What are the personal and social consequences of victimization of the disabled and how can these be ameliorated?

- What is the importance of place and context in understanding crimes against the developmentally disabled, as well as other vulnerable groups, and how can we better understand the dynamics and interaction of caregiver, victim, and context in order to provide improved public safety for this population?
- How can statistics on the victimization of vulnerable populations, including the developmentally disabled, be developed or improved?
- How do the justice and social service systems currently respond to crimes against the developmentally disabled, and how can that response be improved?

Because of the lack of research in this area, the studies of victimization cited by workshop paper authors in this report are few, and most have major methodological flaws. They frequently lack well-designed sampling frames, validated interview methods and protocols, and control groups. For these reasons, no firm conclusions about the major questions contained in the legislation cited above can be drawn from them.

Still, these studies do document a serious victimization problem among people with developmental disabilities. While we cannot draw valid comparisons with victimization rates for other groups, both the nature of the crimes directed against the population with disabilities and the level of harm these crimes inflict suggest to the paper authors and the editors of this report that better research is necessary if society is to protect these most vulnerable citizens. It is in this context that the results of extant research on the victimization of people with disabilities are discussed.

2

Nature and Extent

Although individuals with disabilities have been victimized throughout history, today society is gaining new respect and concern for the civil rights of these vulnerable people. Still, as this process occurs, there are more questions than answers about the nature and extent of criminal victimization of men, women, and children with disabilities. This chapter draws primarily on the workshop papers by Ruth Luckasson, Patricia Sullivan, and Richard McCleary and Douglas Wiebe, as well as the workshop presentation by Mary Ann Curry and Laurie Powers. Brief biographies of the authors of papers summarized in this report can be found in the Appendix.

DEFINITIONS

What Constitutes a Disability?

Disabilities come in many forms, and definitions of disability relate to physical, cognitive, or behavioral characteristics, as well as to an individual's ability to perform specific functions. For example, the ability to see, hear, talk, walk, climb stairs, lift, and carry are considered in some definitions, and the ability to perform the tasks involved in independent living, such as housework, or to participate normally in schooling or other social contexts are considered in others. A person with a severe disability is unable to perform one or more essential activities, requires some kind of assistive device, or needs assistance from another person to perform basic tasks.

Census data from 1994-1995 indicate that about 21 percent of the U.S. population has some form of disability, and that among the 84 million infants, children, and youth ages 0 to 21, 10 percent (8.4 million)—mostly those ages 6 to 14—have a disability. Census data also indicate that among children ages 0 to 14, 1 percent have a severe disability.

Children and youth with emotional and behavioral problems that require residential treatment are a burgeoning population in the United States. Current estimates from the U.S. Department of Health and Human Services (1999) indicate that some 77,200 children and youth reside in psychiatric settings and group homes in this country and that an additional 70 million children and youth are in out-of-home care, including foster care and kinship care. Medical conditions requiring health care have been identified in 60 percent of children placed in foster care; children placed in care due to neglect have the greatest number of medical problems.

On the basis of an analysis of the 1994 National Health Interview Survey-Disability Supplement (NHIS-DS), LaPlante and Carlson (1996) have estimated that 2 percent of the U.S. population has mental retardation or a developmental disability. This is known to be an underestimate, since these data do not include people in institutions, the correctional system, or the military. According to the Arc of the United States—an advocacy organization formerly called Association for Retarded Citizens of the United States—a review of a number of prevalence studies indicates that 2.5 to 3 percent of the general population has mental retardation or a developmental disability (Batshaw, 1997). Applying Batshaw's percentages to the 1990 census of the general population, the Arc of the United States estimates that 6 to 8 million people nationwide have mental retardation (Arc of the United States, 1998).

Definitions Vary

Because of the different definitions of disability, the population with disabilities is difficult to identify, and their victimization is difficult to measure. Different conceptual models have been proposed to understand disability in a variety of domains, especially health, education, and employment. Some of these explanatory paradigms describe disability as a personal problem caused directly by disease or trauma, and for which treatment or a cure is required. In others it is viewed as occurring within a social context; that is, disability is a socially created problem and is in fact a matter of the full integration of individuals into society (World Health Organization, 2000).

The definition in the Crime Victims With Disabilities Awareness Act of 1998 appears comprehensive, but it is not characterized by the clarity and specification required for careful measurement. While the workshop discussion, in part, was organized around the statutory definition, that should not be taken to imply that research, especially the collection of prevalence and incidence data, should be driven by it. In her paper, workshop presenter Patricia Sullivan discusses disability under six categories or explanatory models to help account for differences in definition across the different domains discussed in the literature and embodied in the statutory definition. These categories include the medical model, the educational model, the legal model, the entitlement model, the cultural model, and the integrated model. They vary according to the services or needs of the individual seeking assistance for a particular disability, the needs of those collecting the information, and the estimates they produce of both disability and crime victimization.

These models are not mutually exclusive. For example, both the medical and legal model consider medical and psychiatric problems, and both the educational and medical models consider health-related educational difficulties. The models underscore the problems involved in developing clear definitions on which to base data collection and research efforts. The difficulty of defining disability presents a formidable barrier and challenge to measuring the nature and extent of violence and abuse committed against those with disabilities.

The Medical Model

The medical model of disability pertains to maternal and child health and is predicated on the need to provide some type of health care service to children with developmental disabilities. According to the Bureau of Maternal and Child Health's definition, "children with special health care needs" are children with health problems that require more than routine and basic health care, and they include "children with or at risk of disabilities, chronic illnesses and conditions and health-related education or behavioral problems." The definition also includes "children who have or are at increased risk for chronic physical, developmental, behavioral, or emotional conditions and who also require health and related services of a type or amount beyond that required by children generally."

The Educational Model

The Individuals with Disabilities Education Act of 1997 (P.L. 105-17) mandates a free and appropriate public education for children with disabilities from birth to age 21. The act defines a child with a disability as one with "mental retardation, hearing impairments (including deafness), speech or language impairments, visual impairments (including blindness), serious emotional disturbance, orthopedic impairments, autism, traumatic brain injury, other health impairments, or specific learning disabilities."

Specific learning disability is further defined as "a disorder in one or more of the basic psychological processes involved in understanding or in using language, spoken or written, which disorder may manifest itself in imperfect ability to listen, think, speak, read, write, spell, or do mathematical calculations." The act provides further definitions of the disabilities of infants and toddlers.

During the 1993-1994 school year, some 5 million children and youth with disabilities in the United States received special education services. Children with behavioral/emotional problems, mental retardation, and learning disabilities accounted for 71 percent of the children who received special education services. Speech and language impairments constituted an additional 20 percent of these children with disabilities.

The Legal Model

The Americans with Disabilities Act of 1990 (P.L. 101-336) is the civil rights act of people with disabilities. The framers of this act estimated that some 49 million Americans have some form of disability, and that for 24 million of them, it is severe. Under the act, disability is defined as "a physical or mental impairment that substantially limits one or more of the major life activities of such individual, a record of such an impairment, and being regarded as having such an impairment."

This definition encompasses individuals with mental retardation, hearing impairment, and other health or physical impairments. Psychiatric disorders, such as depression, bipolar disorder, panic and obsessive-compulsive disorders, personality disorders, schizophrenia, and rehabilitation from drug use or addiction, are also included. However, some behavioral syndromes that may be classified as psychiatric disorders are not covered under the Americans with Disabilities Act, and those suffering from them would not be considered people with disabilities. These include sexual behavior disorders, compulsive gambling, kleptomania, pyromania, and current substance abuse. People engaging in these behaviors are not protected by the provisions of the act.

The Entitlement Model

Each year in the United States, Supplemental Social Security Income (SSI) benefits are provided to almost 1 million children age 18 and younger and 7 million adults age 19 and older. The SSI definition of disability for children requires "a child to have a physical or mental condition or conditions that can be medically proven and that result in marked or severe functional limitations." Of the almost 900,000 children with disabilities who receive SSI, the majority live in households in which basic food, clothing, and shelter needs are lacking; some 40 percent are classified as mentally retarded; and 24 percent receive benefits for a mental disorder other than mental retardation.

The Cultural Model

Many individuals with disabilities consider themselves to be members of a minority group. As such, they are a diverse group whose membership numbers 49 million, making it the largest minority in the United States. Deaf and hard-of-hearing people, who represent about 1 percent of the population with disabilities, are unique in that they consider themselves to be a distinct subculture—their community has its own language (American Sign Language), folkways, and a sense of "peoplehood." Many individuals with disabilities prefer not to be categorized in any manner as having a disability.

The Integrated Model

The National Center for Health Statistics houses the information gathered by the National Health Interview Survey on Disability (NHIS-D)—a survey created through the efforts of four federal offices and other organizations interested in maintaining the balance between social, administrative, and medical considerations involved in disability measurement. The survey was designed to collect data that can be used to understand disability, to develop public health policy, to produce simple prevalence estimates of selected health conditions, and to provide descriptive baseline statistics on the effects of disabilities. The survey collects information on childhood disability status, but not on crime victimization, child abuse, or neglect.

International Efforts

The overlapping elements of the various models described in the Sullivan paper are brought together in a classification system developed by the World Health Organization to describe and measure disability in the context of health. The International Classification of Disability and Health (ICIDH-2) has as its overall aim the development of a unified and standard language and framework for the description of health states (including disabilities) for all people. It characterizes the components of health under three constructs: body functions and structures, activities at the individual level (embodying the capacities of individuals), and participation in society, which includes environmental factors or social contexts that influence behavior, ranging from a person's immediate surroundings to the general environment.

While this system can be of utility to statisticians and researchers in their efforts to define developmental and other disabilities, its utility in defining a sampling frame (discussed in Chapter 4) for measuring crime against individuals with disabilities may be limited. This is because the ICIDH-2 does not classify people. Rather it conceives health and disability as a dynamic interaction between health conditions and environmental factors, describing the situation of each person (Internet http://www.who.int/icidh, October 31, 2000).

EXTENT AND NATURE OF CRIMES AGAINST THOSE WITH DISABILITIES

Currently, the two national crime statistics systems in the United States—the Uniform Crime Reports (UCR) of the Federal Bureau of Investigation (FBI) and the National Crime Victimization Survey (NCVS) of the Bureau of Justice Statistics (BJS)—do not identify those with disabilities. Thus, no base rate data on crimes against victims with disabilities are gathered (however, see Chapter 4 for a description of current BJS efforts to address the data collection requirements of the Crime Victims with Disabilities Awareness Act of 1998). In addition, the major child maltreatment databases mandated, compiled, and maintained by the federal government lack data on victimization of children and youth with disabilities. This lack of documentation is a major barrier to understanding the scope and nature of violence and maltreatment of infants, toddlers, children, and youth with disabilities.

Even if the UCR recorded whether the victim had a disability, the data problem would not be solved because most crimes are not reported to the police at all. For example, in 1997, among all populations, only 37 percent of all crimes were reported to the police (Bureau of Justice Statistics, 2000). The percentage is even lower for stigmatized crimes such as sexual assault. Thus the likelihood is low that persons with disabilities report most of the crimes committed against them to the police.

Violent Crimes

Violent crimes committed against people with disabilities include conventional violent crimes (homicide, assault, theft, robbery); abuse, child abuse and neglect (neglect, physical abuse, emotional abuse, and sexual abuse); specialized crimes (abduction by family member, stranger abduction); family violence (domestic violence, spouse abuse, stepparent abuse); and noncriminal violent acts (assaults by other children, sibling assault, bullying, physical interventions/restraint). However, people with disabilities appear to be at higher risks for some types of crime. Anecdotal evidence suggests that they face abnormally high risks of physical and sexual assault and abuse. Studies from Canada, Australia, and Great Britain consistently confirm high rates of violence and abuse by caregivers against people with disabilities. Although there is little empirical research, published findings consistently support the anecdotal evidence.

One review of the available literature concluded as a conservative estimate that people with developmental disabilities are 4 to 10 times more likely to be victims of crimes than other people are (Sobsey et al., 1995). Sobsey and Doe (1991) found that 83 percent of women with intellectual disabilities in their sample had been sexually assaulted and that of those, nearly 50 percent had been sexually assaulted 10 or more times.

A survey of victims of crime administered (with appropriate modifications) by the Australian Bureau of Statistics to a sample of adults with intellectual disabilities found that differences in victimization rates were most pronounced for the crimes of assault (3 times higher than for people without disabilities), sexual assault (11 times higher), and robbery (13 times higher). Only auto theft was lower for the group with disabilities, and that was probably due to the fact that few of them had cars to be stolen. This study also found extremely low rates of reporting to the police: 40 percent of the crimes against people with mild mental retardation went unreported, and 71 percent of those against people with severe mental retardation went unreported (Wilson and Brewer, 1992).

Given the paucity of crime victimization data collected on people with disabilities in general, it is not surprising that minimal research has been conducted on infants, toddlers, children, and youth with disabilities as victims of conventional violent crimes. However, one study of these types of crimes found that high school students with learning disabilities were more likely to be victims of crime (theft and sexual assault) than their peers without such disabilities (Bryan et al., 1989). Another found that students with behavior disorders were more likely to be victims of violent crimes (aggravated assault, robbery, and rape) than their peers who have learning disabilities or mental retardation (Lang and Kahn, 1986). Because these studies included only a small sample and had other limitations, however, it is safe to say that there are essentially no data on the criminal victimization of children with disabilities.

There is also rather limited information on the risk of child abuse among children with disabilities. One study found that children with developmental disabilities were at twice the risk of physical and sexual abuse than children without such disabilities (Crosse et al., 1993). A study for the National Center on Child Abuse and Neglect found that children with disabilities had a 1.7 percent higher risk of maltreatment of all kinds than do other children (Westat, 1993).

Caregiver Violence

Many people with disabilities rely on a paid or unpaid personal assistant to help them with a host of daily activities, ranging from grocery shopping to bathing. There is no national general survey of abuse and violence by caretakers. The one study by the National Institutes of Health identified abuse by attendants and health care providers as a problem and found that women with disabilities are "significantly" more likely to be abused by this population (Young et al., 1997). Although boys and men with disabilities may also experience high rates of abuse from caretakers, there are no data to document this.

One study sought to measure the abuse of women with disabilities by their providers of personal assistance services in an Oregon sample (Curry and Powers, 1999). The researchers divided survey participants into women with a physical disability and those with a developmental disability. Personal assistants were paid or unpaid, including family and friends.

Women with a developmental disability were significantly more likely to report that they had ever experienced several types of abuse, while those with a physical disability were significantly more likely to report that they had experienced abuse within the past year.

Asked about barriers to stopping or preventing abuse, women in both groups identified the same 7 among the top 10 barriers most frequently reported, but in a different order. The seven were: don't know who to call, low personal assistant wages, shortages of personal assistants, no back-up personal assistant, too embarrassed, need help to train personal assistant, and fear personal assistant backlash.

Asked about strategies that might help to stop or prevent abuse by personal assistants, both groups of women mentioned the same 6 strategies in the top 10 but in a different order. The six were: choose own personal assistant, back-up personal assistant available, set limits with personal assistant, clearly stated job description, emergency transportation, and clear communication. Both groups of women ranked the same three strategies as least helpful: call police, use humor during stress, and wait until can act.

Family Violence

Domestic Violence

The problem of domestic violence generally is a well-documented and serious phenomenon in the United States (Rennison and Welchans, 2000; Tjaden and Thoennes, 2000). Moreover, according to the UCR in 1995, female murder victims were more than twice as likely as men to have been killed by husbands or boyfriends. For those cases in which the victim-offender relationship was known, "husbands or boyfriends killed 26 percent of female murder victims, whereas wives or girlfriends killed 3 percent of the male victims" (Craven, 1996:2). The same report said that women experienced seven times as many incidents of nonfatal violence by an intimate as did males.

Given this, it seems obvious that women with disabilities would also be victims of this type of crime (McPherson, 1991), but there is no similar documentation of the victimization of this vulnerable population. None of the national surveys addresses whether or not female victims have a disability, and the studies that have been done with the population of women with disabilities mostly combine all violence (domestic violence, rape, sexual assault, stranger assault) and do not distinguish whether it was committed by an intimate partner (Nosek and Howland, 1998).

About a half-dozen studies look at the subject of physical assaults against women with disabilities. Their estimations of the prevalence of some type of physical or emotional abuse at the hands of an intimate partner or caregiver range from 39 to 85 percent. A study of 245 women with disabilities by the Disabled Women's Network of Canada in 1989 found that 40 percent had experienced abuse (Nosek and Howland, 1998). The Canadian National Clearinghouse on Family Violence reports on a study that found that 40 percent of women with disabilities had been assaulted, raped or abused, and 39 percent of ever-married women with a disability had been physically or sexually assaulted by their partners (Roeher Institute, 1994). The National Institutes of Health studied 860 women, 439 of whom were disabled and found matching levels of reported physical abuse (36 percent in both groups) and sexual abuse (40 percent of women with disabilities and 37 percent of women without disabilities), but the length of time abuse was experienced was longer for women with disabilities—3.9 years compared with 2.5 years on average (Young et al., 1997). The Colorado Department of Health reported that 85 percent of women with disabilities are victims of abuse (Tyiska, 1998).

Most of these studies do not separate out abuse by an intimate partner and abuse by a nonintimate caregiver and do not distinguish between types of abuse committed (e.g., physical, verbal). As noted earlier, only the National Institutes of Health broke down abuse by attendants and health care providers and found that women with disabilities are "significantly" more likely to be abused by this population (Young et al., 1997).

Erwin (1999) notes that once in an abusive relationship, women with disabilities are motivated to stay by the same host of factors that keep other women in these relationships: fear of further violence, belief that the batterer will change, love of the abuser, having children in common, having no economic support if they leave, and religious beliefs, in addition to other concerns. But for women with disabilities, additional factors can limit their ability to leave, such as physically not being able to exit the house, fear of losing caregiver service if they report the abuse, not knowing if the local shelter is physically accessible (i.e., wheelchair ramp, workers who know sign language), fear they will be institutionalized if they leave their partner, and lack of resources.

The latter is particularly important, since many women with disabilities either do not work at all or do not work full time. The unemployment rate of women with disabilities is reported to be 74 percent, and those who do work earn only 64 percent of the wages of women without disabilities (Burstow, 1992). Magnifying all of these issues is the fact that society's message to women with disabilities is they are lucky to have a partner at all (McPherson, 1991). Fear of losing that status may keep many of these women from reporting abusive behavior by their partner.

Severity of Abuse

The Office of Victims of Crime reports that catastrophic injuries as the result of violent assaults can result in loss of abilities to see, hear, touch, taste, feel, move, and think in the usual ways (Tyiska, 1998). A report by the National Clearinghouse on Family Violence (1998) in Canada reports that women have cited violence by their husbands as causing a loss of vision and a loss of mobility. The range of disabilities resulting from abuse go from actual physical disabilities to more hidden trauma, including head injuries, cognitive problems, and posttraumatic stress disorder (PTSD) (Koss et al., 1994; Tjaden and Thoennes, 2000).

A 1995 study examined the prevalence of PTSD in battered women (Kemp et al., 1995). The results showed that 81 percent of the subjects who were physically battered had a diagnosis of PTSD, while 63 percent of those who suffered only verbal abuse met the same criteria. The physically battered women with PTSD reported more physical and verbal abuse, more injuries, a greater sense of threat, and more forced sex in the relationship than did their verbally abused counterparts. The authors concluded that battered women, particularly those who experience extensive physical abuse, are at risk for posttraumatic stress disorder. Because this study was not longitudinal and involved retrospective self-reports regarding the severity of abuse, it is difficult to determine whether the posttraumatic stress disorder was present in some subjects before the abuse occurred or resulted from some other trauma.

This information is clearly not conclusive, and more research is needed to determine how many women who are victims of domestic violence suffer either permanent or temporary disability as a result of the battering and the type of disability.

Child Abuse and Neglect

Over the past 30 years, interest in child abuse and neglect has led researchers to study the relationships between disability, child abuse, and neglect. The following section describes the limited research in this area, drawing on the paper prepared for the workshop by Patricia Sullivan.

Professionals, including child protection workers and educators, believe that children with disabilities are at high risk for abuse and that some disabilities are caused or exacerbated by abuse (Schilling et al., 1986; Sobsey, 1994; Sobsey and Varnhagen, 1988). However, there is a surprising paucity of methodologically sound research in the field of child abuse and disability (Ammerman, 1991; Knutson, 1988; Knutson and Schartz, 1997). Existing literature addressing the problem of abuse and the disabled can be categorized under three major headings: (1) the perception of high incidence rates of victimization among children with disabilities, (2) the proportion of children with disabilities within a sample of abuse victims, and (3) the proportion of abuse victims within a sample of children with disabilities.

Perception of High Prevalence Rates

Because of their vulnerability and greater need for care, children with disabilities are presumed to be at higher risk for abuse by parents and other caregivers than are other children. For example, some authors argue that children with mental retardation are at greater risk because ordinary standards of care are inadequate for them (Schilling and Schinke, 1984) and because they are less protected by the incest taboo than are other children (Neutra et al., 1977). Many children with disabilities exhibit behavioral characteristics, such as tantrums, aggressiveness, and noncompliance, that negatively affect their parents and caregivers, increasing the risk of abuse (Solomons, 1979). Finally, various disabilities, including mental retardation (Sangrund et al., 1974), cerebral palsy (Jaudes and Diamond, 1985), developmental delays (Augoustinos, 1987), speech and language disabilities (Fox et al., 1988; Law and Conway, 1992), and multiple-personality disorders (Putnam et al., 1986), have been attributed to abuse and neglect.

Specific caretaking roles required for some disabilities may create a context that increases the risk of abuse. One study found, for example, that the majority of day care abuse occurs around toileting (Finkelhor et al., 1988), suggesting to some that a need for toileting assistance may be associated with increased risk of sexual abuse for people with disabilities. Residential placement may also provide opportunity for abuse by caretakers. For example, a study of deaf youth found that sexual abuse tended to occur as a result of caretaker access to residents in private settings, such as bathrooms and bedrooms, at residential educational facilities (Sullivan et al., 1987).

Disabilities in Samples of Maltreated Children

Studies have found highly variable prevalence rates of disabilities in samples of abused and neglected children and youth, ranging from a low of 22 percent to a high of 70 percent (22 percent in Gil, 1970; 26 percent in Birrell and Birrell, 1968; 43 percent in Lightcap et al., 1982; 66 percent in Mian et al., 1986; 70 percent in Johnson and Morse, 1968). Among incest victims, high incidences of abnormal EEGs and disabling conditions have also been reported (Browning and Boatman, 1977; Davies, 1979). In a West Virginia sample of identified child abuse cases, 70 percent were found to have disabilities and 35 percent had disabilities attributed to maltreatment (Souther, 1986). Differences in criteria used for determining abuse and disability among the studies almost certainly contribute to the wide range of findings.

Only seven states collect information on the special characteristics, including disabilities, of abused and neglected children (Bonner et al., 1997). Although the majority of child protective service workers believe that children with disabilities are at increased risk for maltreatment, most have never served clients with disabilities and are not trained to effectively diagnose disabilities (Schilling et al., 1986).

Abuse Among Samples of Children with Disabilities

Prevalence rates of sexual abuse among the mentally retarded have been found to range from a low of 3 percent (Hard, 1986) to a high of 25 percent (Chamberlain et al., 1984). Sexual abuse rates of 20 percent have been reported in children with cerebral palsy (Diamond and Jaudes, 1983) and of 23 to 50 percent for hearing-impaired children (Sullivan et al., 1987). One study also found that children with less severe developmental impairments were at greater risk for abuse.

Several studies of abuse and neglect among samples of children and adults with disabilities referred to treatment centers have been conducted.

This research is limited by subject selection bias, in that subjects obtained from hospitals, medical treatment centers, or institutions for people with disabilities cannot be considered representative of all children with disabilities; thus these findings cannot be considered definitive. Nevertheless, these studies suggest that abuse prevalence rates may be high among children and youth with disabilities.

For example, Sullivan et al. (1991) investigated patterns of abuse among a sample of 482 consecutively referred maltreated children with disabilities in a hospital setting. Results indicated that sexual abuse or a combination of sexual and physical abuse were the most common forms of maltreatment the children experienced. The majority of subjects had communication disorders, including speech or hearing impairments, learning disabilities, and cleft lip or palate. Males with disabilities were more likely to be victims of sexual abuse than males in the general population, and placement in a residential school was identified as a major risk factor for sexual abuse among youngsters with disabilities.

These studies were replicated in a five-year retrospective study of 4,340 child patients in a pediatric hospital. In that setting, 68 percent were found to be victims of sexual abuse and 32 percent were victims of physical abuse (Willging et al., 1992). Studies in Great Britain (Westcott, 1991), Australia (Turk and Brown, 1992), and Canada (Sobsey and Doe, 1991) have found that sexual abuse is the most prevalent form of maltreatment among children with disabilities.

Epidemiological Studies

Several epidemiological studies of children address the links between disability and maltreatment from different perspectives, using control groups. They were completed at the Center for Abused Children with Disabilities at the Boys Town National Research Hospital.

In the first, a hospital-based study examining the prevalence of disabilities among maltreated versus nonmaltreated children, researchers merged more than 39,000 hospital records from 10 years (1982 to 1992) with the social service central registry, the foster care review board, and police records to identify cases of both intrafamilial and extrafamilial maltreatment (Sullivan and Knutson, 1998a). The merger resulted in more than 6,000 matches and an overall maltreatment prevalence rate of 15 percent. Among the 15 percent of children identified as maltreated, 64 percent had a disability, whereas only 32 percent of the nonmaltreated children had a disability. Identified disabilities included behavior disorders (38 percent); speech/language disorders (9 percent); mental retardation (6 percent); hearing impairment (6 percent); learning disability (6 percent); other disabilities (4 percent); health impairments (2 percent); and attention deficit disorder without conduct disorder (2 percent).

A second study that drew its sample from public and parochial school populations permitted prevalence estimates of abuse among children with disabilities based on standard definitions of the various forms of maltreatment and homogeneous education-based definitions of disabilities. The school-based study merged almost 50,000 records from Omaha public and parochial schoolchildren matriculated during the 1994-1995 school year with the Nebraska central registry of abuse and neglect cases, the foster care review board, and Omaha police records of child maltreatment (Sullivan and Knutson, 1999b). From this merger, 4,954 children were identified as maltreated, 11 percent in the public schools and 5 percent in parochial schools. In contrast, 31 percent of the children with an identified disability had records of maltreatment in either social services or police agencies. The relative risk for maltreatment among children with disabilities was found to be three times that of other children. Overall, there was a strong association between disabilities and neglect, with children with disabilities being four times more likely to be victims of neglect than other children. Children with behavior disorders and mental disabilities were significantly more likely to be neglected than children with other disabilities.

The results of this research suggested to the researchers the need for longitudinal studies related to domestic violence and disability status.

Noncriminal Violent Acts

Noncriminal violent acts include assault by peers, sibling assault, bullying, and condoned physical interventions, which can escalate to abuse. In one hospital-based epidemiological study (Sullivan and Knutson, 1998a), a peer physical abuse rate of 3 percent was found among victims with disabilities. Siblings also are involved in physical abuse and peers and siblings account for a small percentage of sexual abuse of children with disabilities as well. Bullying of children and youth with disabilities has been addressed empirically in the United Kingdom and other European countries (Dawkins, 1996; Roland and Munthe, 1989). Defined as physical or psychological teasing, name-calling, hitting, pushing, social exclusion, threats, extortion, and theft, bullying is considered a form of peer abuse. Dawkins

(1996) found that children enrolled in special education programs associated with visible disabilities, such as cerebral palsy, blindness, and deafness, were twice as likely to be bullied as children with disabilities not associated with visible physical conditions, such as learning disabilities and behavior disorders; some 33 percent of these children were regularly bullied at school, with boys being bullied more than girls.

Currently, it is not known whether children and youth with disabilities have a higher base rate of these noncriminal types of violence than their peers without disabilities.

Disabilities as a Consequence of Criminal Victimization

Disabilities can also result from the experience of violence or some form of child maltreatment. Although data are limited on the prevalence of acquired disabilities, given the problem of determining the temporal association between the onset of the disability and the occurrence of the violent act, it is estimated that 33 percent of all spinal cord injuries are the result of intentional violence (Waters et al., 1996), although it is not known if there were other preexisting disabilities among those who suffered spinal cord injury.

Traumatic brain injury is the most devastating type of pediatric trauma. Each year, an estimated 50,000 children and adolescents sustain permanent disability as the result of brain injury (Stylianos, 1998). Unfortunately, follow-up data on the nature and extent of the child's disability status typically do not cover events beyond the resolution of the acute trauma.

Institutional Abuse

Approximately 2 percent of the 4.5 million children and youth with disabilities in the United States live in institutions, including nursing homes; schools for the blind, deaf, and physically disabled; institutions for the mentally retarded; and facilities for the mentally ill. Some research has found residential placement to be a risk factor for experiencing sexual or physical abuse (Brookhouser, 1987; Sullivan et al., 1987; Sullivan and Knutson, 1998b; Sullivan et al., 1999a), but there remains very little empirical data on victimization in institutional settings.

BARRIERS TO OBTAINING INFORMATION

In her presentation, Sullivan noted several significant challenges facing researchers who attempt to study victimization of children and adults with disabilities. First, crime victimization and child maltreatment may be both risks and consequences of disability status. Second, risk factors and consequences appear to vary as a function of the type of crime, the type of maltreatment, and the type of disability. Third, many levels of information exist regarding crimes against people with disabilities, but prevalence estimates are only as good as the information in the estimate source. Fourth, at this time, it is impossible to link data from disability sources to criminal justice and health-related databases. Further discussion of the difficulties of gathering victimization data from people with disabilities is covered in Chapter 4 on measuring victimization.

Available data on abuse among people with disabilities are problematic because of the differing operational definitions of maltreatment, poorly defined heterogeneous populations with disabilities, and questionable validation procedures for determining disabilities (Ammerman et al., 1988; Knutson, 1988; Knutson and Schartz, 1997). For children, merely using central registries of child abuse and neglect to establish a link between abuse and disabilities will not alleviate the problem. Abuse records of children are not systematically entered among states, and extrafamilial abuse is not included in virtually any central registry (Flango, 1988). Furthermore, many incidents of maltreatment known to professionals and lay persons are not reported to appropriate agencies, which leads to underestimates of true levels of maltreatment (Knutson, 1988).

Another problem is that disabling conditions can be conceptualized as chronic stressors for care providers, as well as disrupters of the attachment process, because disabilities can cause people to be difficult to manage, to evidence significant cognitive impairments, to be communicatively limited, or to be limited in mobility. Unfortunately, virtually all disabling conditions or their behavioral manifestations can also be occasioned by physical abuse or neglect. As a result, it is often impossible to determine whether the disability contributes to abuse or whether it is a consequence of abuse. Thus, there is controversy regarding disabilities as a risk factor in abuse.

3

Risk Factors for People with Disabilities

People with disabilities may be particularly vulnerable to crimes involving interpersonal violence, such as physical or sexual assault, because as a population—regardless of age or gender—they are often the least able to recognize danger, the least able to protect themselves, and the least able to obtain assistance within the criminal justice system. By the same token, they may be less vulnerable than the rest of the population to other crimes, for example, auto theft, since few of them own vehicles.

This chapter presents the multifactorial model of the risk of violence directed at people with disabilities posited by Dick Sobsey and Peter Calder in their workshop paper. The authors discussed the risk of victimization for persons with disabilities in a historical context of victimization studies generally. Their model is grounded in the fragile empirical research and case study material partially summarized in Chapter 2, but because of the lack of empirically tested risk factors to explain the increased incidence of violence against people with disabilities, the elements of the conceptual model should be considered as theoretical and untested. Still, the model integrates a wide range of concepts, models, and theories into a rational organizational structure, with five goals:

1. to summarize the specific risk factors that affect people with disabilities;
2. to provide a basis for discussing the development of a more refined model or a better alternative model;

3. to call for the generation of testable hypotheses based on various components of the model;
4. to provide a tentative guide for risk reduction strategies; and
5. to consider the specific risk factors and mechanisms that affect people with disabilities in order to further understanding of violence and violence prevention in general.

Significant studies of crime victims began in the middle of the 20th century. Like much of the work that followed, early studies in victimology emphasized the importance of considering the relationship between the perpetrator and the victim. Von Hentig (1948) is credited with first identifying the relationship between disability and victimization when he suggested that four categories of people are particularly vulnerable to victimization: the young, the old, females, and the mentally disabled. However, the relationship between disabilities and crime victimization received little attention until the 1960s when studies found high rates of developmental, physical, and behavioral disabilities among abused children (see, e.g., Birrell and Birrell, 1968; Elmer and Gregg, 1967; Gil, 1970; Johnson and Morse, 1968). Studies that followed also revealed higher than expected rates of substantiated child abuse among children with disabilities (e.g., Buchanan and Oliver, 1977; Frisch and Rhoads, 1982). These studies demonstrated a relationship between abuse and disability, but they shed little light on why the relationship might exist or whether disability was an outcome of or a risk factor for abuse.

The traditional explanation for seemingly high rates of child abuse and other forms of violence against people with disabilities is referred to as the dependency-stress model. Used extensively between the 1960s and the 1990s, this model is fashioned on several premises: children with disabilities are more dependent on their caregivers; increased dependency increases the demands on caregivers; increased demands result in increased stress for caregivers; and caregivers abuse their charges because they cannot cope with the increased stress. Although this model appears to be logical, little research supports it, and some research seems to contradict it altogether (e.g., Benedict et al., 1992; Pillemer and Finkelhor, 1989; Starr et al., 1984). Furthermore, the model can be construed as excusing offenders or even transforming them into victims while blaming the real victims for causing stress.

THE MULTIFACTORIAL MODEL OF VIOLENCE

In the past 40 years, researchers, family members, caregivers, and others have gained better understanding of the cognitive and physical abilities of people with developmental disabilities. As many of them have moved from institutions to partly and sometimes almost fully independent lifestyles, researchers have gained a broader understanding of the complexity of violent victimization within this population and a view that no existing model fully explains why these individuals are victimized.

In their paper written for the workshop, Sobsey and Calder propose that explaining victimization requires an examination of a number of factors. Their multifactorial model synthesizes existing models and elements, drawing specifically on three models from other domains: (1) the counter-control model, which is used to analyze social interaction in behavioral psychology; (2) the lifestyles or routine activities model, which is frequently discussed in criminology; and (3) the ecological model, which is commonly used in discussions of child abuse. In addition, their model incorporates victim-related factors, offender-related factors, relationship factors, and environmental factors. The following section summarizes these models from other domains and suggests their relevance to people with disabilities, then explains the additional factors that make up the multifactorial model.

Contributions from Other Domains

Counter-Control Model

According to the behavioral model of counter-control, when one individual exerts control over another, the second individual responds with counter-control. Thus, victimization can be predicted on the basis of the relative power of individuals and groups of individuals. From this perspective, people with disabilities would be victimized more frequently than others because they lack power and are less successful at recruiting assistance from more powerful protectors.

Routine Activities or Lifestyle Model

The premise of routine activities or lifestyle model is that the characteristics of potential victims influence role expectation and structural constraints to which they must adapt. These adaptations combine with the role of expectations and structural constraints to influence daily routines or lifestyles. Lifestyle, in turn, determines the degree of exposure to potential offenders—the greater the exposure, the greater the risk of victimization. The model identifies several conditions that must occur for a crime to take place: exposure of the potential victim to the offender, motivation to commit the crime by the potential offender, a willingness to use criminal means to attain that end by the potential offender, and the potential offender's belief that the desired end can be achieved without paying too severe a penalty.

This model suggests a number of possible explanations for the risk of victimization of people with disabilities. For example, institutional care may function both to increase the exposure of people with disabilities to potential offenders and may isolate them from sources of protection, such as the police. An offender may choose an individual with a disability as a victim out of a belief that apprehension is less likely and that punishment will be less severe if apprehension occurs.

Combining the counter-control theory with this lifestyle model raises the hypothesis that institutionalization not only increases exposure to risk, but also increases the power differential by defining the roles of people with disabilities and staff in a manner that magnifies power differences.

The Ecological Model

The ecological model was developed by Bronfenbrenner (1977) to analyze child development. Used extensively to analyze healthy and abusive relationships between children and their caregivers, it provides a framework to analyze abuse of children with disabilities and violence against adults with disabilities. According to this model, violence or abuse is one form of interaction between two individuals—the offender and the victim. Their relationship is referred to as a microsystem—the child with a disability and his parent, the adult with a disability and his or her personal care provider. The model stresses that this relationship exists with and is strongly influenced by a unit of the social environment—a family, a group home, an institution—that is in turn strongly influenced by the society or culture. The attitudes and beliefs of a culture, for example, might determine whether or not an act is considered to be a crime, the priority it will be given for investigation, and the severity of the sentence that might be applied.

A variation of the ecological model has been adapted to explain victimization of people with disabilities (Sobsey, 1994).

Components of the Multifactorial Model

The multifactorial model expands on the ecological model by incorporating the counter-control and routine activities models. The potential victim, the potential offender, inhibition and disinhibition within the offender, interactions between the potential victim and potential offender and the relationship that determines those interactions—social control agents, the environment in which interactions occur, and the culture of the society that influences every interaction within it—these are the primary components of the multifactorial model and the primary factors that contribute to the increased risk of violence experienced by people with disabilities.

Victim-Related Factors

In attempting to understand why individuals with disabilities are victimized, some prefer not to examine the role of the victim, believing that such an examination shifts blame from the offender. Victimology, the study of the characteristics and behavior of people who are victimized, is relevant, however, for several reasons: evidence that blaming the victim is common is considerable; total denial that victim attributes and behavior influence risk suggests that individuals are powerless to reduce their risk; and evidence shows that factors such as age, gender, lifestyle, socioeconomic status, and disability affect the risk of victimization. Thus, exploring and understanding the reasons for differential risk may help to reduce risk for vulnerable members of society.

Direct Effects of Disability A disability can directly affect the capacity of individuals to protect themselves, to avoid or escape from victimization, and to seek help. Some disabilities also increase dependency on caregivers. These effects of disability in increasing risk are minimal for very young children (because all young children are extremely limited in these abilities), but they become increasingly important in older children and adults. In addition, some disabilities impair judgment. People with developmental or psychiatric disabilities often have difficulty identifying when to be compliant and when to assert themselves. As a result, they may be victimized both when they comply too easily and when their refusal to comply provokes retaliation.

Socially Mediated Effects of Disability People with disabilities are often taught unquestioning compliance but rarely taught assertiveness and choice making. In addition, Sobsey and Calder maintain, they are rarely taught their human and civil rights; frequently taught to respond in the same way to a large number of caregivers rather than distinguishing family members and others from strangers; often denied appropriate sex education; often taught passive communication strategies but few social control functions; and often taught through physical prompting that does not allow for the development of an age-appropriate sense of personal space, which may be perceived as vulnerability by sexual offenders. These teachings or omissions in education put individuals with disabilities at risks that are not inherent to the individual or the disability.

Victim Precipitation Victims sometimes exhibit behaviors that elicit violence on the part of the perpetrator. This does not mean, however, that the violence is justified by the behavior or that the violence was intended to be criminal. For instance, an individual with a developmental disability was beaten by police when he was mistaken for a robber who was resisting arrest because he did not communicate with the arresting officers (*St. Louis Post-Dispatch*, 1998).

Persons with developmental disabilities may have difficulty recognizing situations in which danger exists and therefore may be less likely to take precautions. These victim-precipitation factors are likely to interact with offender disinhibitions, particularly when the atypical behavior associated with some disabilities requires caregiver intervention.

Attractive Victims Although perceived vulnerability is a factor in the selection of an individual with a developmental disability as a victim, vulnerability by itself is rarely, if ever, sufficient to motivate a crime. The potential victim must have something the offender wants or have the ability to produce an event the offender finds desirable. Motivating factors include:

- **Control over the victim.** Many crimes against people with disabilities are related to coercion or punishment in an effort to gain control over the victim's behavior (see, e.g., *Cincinnati Enquirer*, 1997; *Hartford Courant*, 1998).
- **Sex.** Sexual offenses against people with disabilities appear to be common. In some cases, offenders have a special sexual attraction to people

with specific disabilities. Others may have a need to direct sexual aggression toward individuals they consider to be vulnerable.

- **Money.** In some cases, people with disabilities may stand between offenders and a large amount of money. Caregivers of individuals with disabilities have been known to kill their charges to gain control of money left by parents for the ongoing care of their offspring; medical negligence or other court awards; insurance settlements; life insurance policies; social security benefits; and the like (see, e.g., Norton, 1994). More commonly, however, such caregiver-offenders simply keep their victims alive in a state of fear and neglect, making money by collecting rent and other fees from them.
- **Few alternatives to exploitation.** Victims of violence who have disabilities sometimes allow themselves to remain in risky situations or to be victimized because life offers them few alternatives. For example, an abusive caretaker may be retained because no one else can be found.

Offender-Related Factors

In many instances, offenders target individuals with developmental disabilities because of their perceptions of them as vulnerable, their personality profile, or their lack of training in the care of individuals with disabilities. In addition, some offenders are themselves afflicted with a developmental disability. Specific offender-related factors in the victimization of people with developmental disabilities are discussed in the following sections.

Perceived Vulnerability The perception that disability increases vulnerability may add to the risk of victimization. Perceived vulnerability refers to the potential offender's estimation of a potential victim's vulnerability. It may be based, in part, on actual vulnerability or on a misperception of vulnerability. In either case, an attractive victim is one who appears vulnerable to the offender. Media portrayals of people with disabilities may add to this perception of vulnerability (see, e.g., Senn, 1988). Some movies portray persons with a vision, hearing, or other disability as helpless victims of predators.

Profiles of Offenders Some authors suggest that at least some offenders against people with developmental disabilities fit specific profiles. Sobsey (1994) outlines two basic profiles for caregiver offenders, and MacNamara

(1992) lists a number of possible patterns. These profiles apply mainly to paid and volunteer caregivers. One study found that 44 percent of the offenders in its sample against people with disabilities made initial contact with their victims through the web of special services provided to people with disabilities (Sobsey and Doe, 1991).

Predatory Caregivers Predatory caregivers seek or maintain employment as caregivers in order to have access to victims. These individuals typically commit offenses with greater elements of planning and organization, although they may also commit impulsive offenses if their authority is threatened. Their offenses may include extreme physical or sexual violence or may be limited to simple harassment and degradation of the victim. The profile of many of these offenders is an individual with overwhelming feelings of inadequacy, lack of control over others, and an overwhelming need to assert control over others seen as vulnerable. For these offenders, control can take the form of bondage, torture, sexual assault, or a variety of other actions.

Corrupted Caregivers This type of caregiver typically does not plan to offend. Under some conditions, they may even be acceptable or very good caregivers. Lack of adequate training, supervision, or clear policy results in the development of abusive patterns of interaction by these individuals.

At some point in their caregiving activities, most caregivers experience inappropriate feelings—anger or even sexual attraction toward a client. Most recognize that acting on those feelings is wrong, but some will cross the boundaries into offensive behavior. Often these offenders are corrupted gradually, in stages, but sometimes the deterioration is sudden—for instance, a resident with a disability slaps or spits at the caregiver and the caregiver explodes into a violent rage.

Offenders with Disabilities Sometimes crimes against people with disabilities are committed by others with disabilities. Much of this can be explained by a lifestyles exposure model, that is, the clustering of people with disabilities into group living situations increases the exposure of potential victims with disabilities to potential offenders with disabilities. Two mechanisms may increase offensive behavior on the part of some people with disabilities. First, residents who have been abused by staff may go on to abuse other residents. Second, some disabilities result in damage to areas of the brain that control impulsive behavior, which can lead directly to lack of inhibition and a greater probability of offending.

Relationship Factors

Many individuals with developmental disabilities must depend on caregivers to a greater extent than other individuals of a similar age. This dependence on others may result in power inequities, and power inequities tend to increase the possibility of abuse (Sobsey, 1994). In addition, people with disabilities may be exposed to a large number of caregivers because of the care requirements of the disability and the turnover in staff of service delivery systems. Exposure to large numbers of caregivers increases the risk that at least one may become abusive (Sobsey, 1994).

Healthy bonds with family members and other intimates provide a significant barrier to abuse and violence. Circumstances that commonly accompany disability may threaten or disrupt attachment and bonding. For instance, treatment of health problems may limit parent-child interactions. Moreover, parents are often implicitly and sometimes explicitly told that it is better not to get too attached to a child with a disability and that such a child will strain their marriage, career, happiness, and sanity. These negative expectations may interfere with parent-child bonding.

Environmental Factors

Environmental factors can both lead to developmental disabilities and increase the risk of violence against those with disabilities. Sobsey and Calder noted as examples the following environmental factors:

- Many people have disabilities that result, in whole or in part, from violence or severe neglect that caused physical damage or permanent neurological changes. Often such violence comes from the victim's own family or community and, unless the victim is removed, continues to put him or her at risk.
- Children born to mothers with severe substance abuse problems or who have endured spousal abuse during pregnancy may be likely to be born with developmental disabilities. Children born into families in which violence was present before their birth are more likely to become abused children.
- Families of people with disabilities may become isolated from their

communities and extended families, which increases the risk of violence. Group homes and institutions can also be isolating.

- Alternative living situations may cluster vulnerable individuals with those who are likely to abuse them without providing safeguards against victimization.
- Foster care homes, group homes, and institutions have all been found to increase the risks of victimization compared with typical natural families.
- Adults, adolescents, and even some children without disabilities have often been able to escape from abusive living alternatives by making other life choices. People with disabilities are often prevented from making such choices.
- Disabilities affect routine activities and exposure to high-risk environments. Many people who have development disabilities do not drive and are therefore much more likely to rely on mass transportation, walking, or others to get where they need to go. One study analyzing patterns of the sexual abuse of children with disabilities and the sexual assault of adults with disabilities found that 5 percent of offenses were committed by specialized transportation providers and 10 percent of offenses took place in vehicles (Sobsey and Doe, 1991). In addition, people are often committed to institutional care because they are unable to look after themselves or because they are dangerous to others. As a result, possible victims and prospective offenders are placed in close proximity with inadequate safeguards.

A STARTING POINT

This chapter presents a model developed by Sobsey and Calder to explain the perceived disproportionate victimization of people with developmental disabilities. They suggest a long list of potential mechanisms that may contribute to the increased risk of violence and abuse for people with disabilities. The list is not comprehensive and the research that supports it is limited, but the mechanisms described here do represent a starting point. In their paper, Sobsey and Calder conclude that research would be required to determine which of these—or which other—mechanisms play a significant role in the victimization of people with disabilities.

4

Measurement Issues

Congress has called on the Bureau of Justice Statistics to measure crime against those with disabilities using the National Crime Victimization Survey (NCVS). Drawing from the paper by Richard McCleary and Douglas Wiebe, this chapter examines some of the methodological challenges involved in adapting extant surveys, such as the NCVS, to people with disabilities. Specifically, we address potential biases introduced by the sample design and methodological difficulties associated with interview methods.

For example, it is important to remember that criminal victimization of the types counted in the NCVS is relatively rare, that is, in any given reference period, the vast majority of respondents do not report any victimization. Very large household samples are therefore required for reliable estimates, and detailed subgroup analyses are problematic. For a variety of reasons, some important subgroups are not covered at all, and smaller research studies of crimes against these subgroups often have problems of statistical power because of small sample sizes in most cases. Furthermore, as with most crime surveys, the NCVS involves self-reports from victims, a method that presents a range of methodological challenges, for example, with regard to standard definitions of events, and the asking of sensitive questions. Although the methodological issues involved in measuring victimization are well known, new ones will emerge when data from the subpopulation of persons with disabilities are integrated. In their paper, McCleary and Wiebe examine the current state of knowledge, outline a set of emerging methodological issues, and discuss potential solutions to the implied validity problems. This chapter summarizes these themes.

Although all people with disabilities are of interest in this context, the discussions here are limited to the methodological issues associated with the integration of people with developmental disabilities, because each subpopulation of people with disabilities—cognitive, sensory, and physical—poses unique problems that alone would warrant a book-length essay.

SAMPLE DESIGN ISSUES

The Sample Frame

The first step in designing a sample is to define the population and the sample frame. In the case of people with developmental disabilities, the difficulty is to construct a list of sampling units—a frame. For example, the sampling frame for the NCVS is all U.S. households from which a nationally representative sample of 50,000 U.S. households comprising nearly 100,000 people is drawn. From this frame large segments of the general population, such as men, women, the elderly, and some minority groups such as blacks and Hispanics, can be identified, and the frequency characteristics and consequences of their victimization experiences can be explored through interviews. In the case of people with developmental disabilities, however, there is no exhaustive list that could serve as a sample frame. Household lists (of addresses, phone numbers, etc.) are problematic because a large proportion of this population does not reside in household units but in institutions, intermediate care facilities, and the like, so household lists would miss them. While this difficulty might be overcome, locating the population that resides in households also would require that the household member who answers the telephone or door identify a resident with a developmental disability as such. Many individuals with developmental disabilities will not admit having a disability, and some individuals without developmental disabilities will say they have a disability, causing incorrect households to be identified (see section below on screening bias).

The problems of using existing nonhousehold lists of persons with developmental disabilities are illustrated by the Client Development Evaluation Reports (CDERs) in California. In that state, an annual evaluation of each person with a developmental disability results in a CDER report. With some difficulty, these reports can be linked over time for tracking or monitoring individuals, or they can be arrayed in a cross-section for measuring the prevalence of developmental disabilities. (Although CDERs have a wealth of clinical information and other data, they contain no information of victimization experience.) As a sample frame, CDERs are limited both because they do not include every person in the state with a developmental disability (enrollment in the state system is voluntary), and because funding exigencies may bias data in other unknown ways. When a group of researchers from UCI Mental Retardation Research Center investigated the adequacy of CDERs for program evaluation, they found that only 3,067 of the 8,502 patients listed in a centralized medical reimbursement database could be located in CDERs. Thus, this reporting system is not a reliable sample frame.

Screening Bias

In the case of developmental disabilities, screening is likely to yield a biased overestimate of the disability-specific victimization rate because of the rarity of a particular disability. As Hemenway (1997:1434) noted: "No matter how specific the test, if the population is at low risk for having the disease, results that are positive will most likely be false positive. With a huge number of actual negatives, virtually any screen or screening question will pick up a sizeable absolute number of false positives."

Thus, McCleary and Wiebe concluded, if items were added to the NCVS to screen for developmental disabilities, a large majority of the self-identified population of persons with developmental disabilities would be false positives. Because these respondents would presumably have lower risks of victimization, the screening items would bias the relative risk of victimization toward zero.

INTERVIEW METHODS

Although the methodological problems associated with sampling can be nearly insurmountable for a survey, in many respects, they are minor compared with the methodological problems associated with interviewing. Specifically, within this population group, three serious problems, according to McCleary and Wiebe, are incidence of caretaker-perpetrated victimizations, the widespread use of proxy respondents, and a wide variety of language and communication disabilities among the victimized population that may require individualized interviewing techniques.

Caregiver-Perpetrated Victimization

Conventional approaches to estimating the victimization risk of persons with developmental disabilities require the active cooperation of caretakers. A major problem of assessing victimization is that the victim may know the perpetrator and may be unwilling to report the event for fear of his or her reprisal. For example, O'Brien (1985) found in rape incidents that this fear may depend on the proximity of the relationship between the perpetrator and victim. The likelihood of a rape being reported is less if the perpetrator and victim are acquainted (51 percent) than if the perpetrator is a stranger (66 percent), and less still if the perpetrator and victim are related (44 percent).

A general unwillingness of people with disabilities to disclose victimization to anyone may be especially problematic because many of the crimes against them may be committed by known offenders on whom they depend for assistance. For instance, when Sobsey (1994) examined offender-victim relationships with data from the University of Alberta Abuse and Disability Project, he found that among 215 cases of abuse among adults with a developmental disability, 52 percent were victimized by someone who was associated through contact with disability services. Other research has also found that a large proportion of victimizations are committed by service providers and family members and by peers with disabilities. Turk and Brown (1992) found that 58 percent of offenses against adults with disabilities occurred in the home of either the victim (48 percent) or the perpetrator (10 percent). Because many surveys, including the NCVS, are conducted from the respondent's home, where perpetrators may be within earshot, victimization may go unreported.

Proxy Respondents

Proxy interviews are often used as a tool to help obtain interviews from individuals who would otherwise be excluded from a survey or from types of individuals who would be underrepresented in a sample. The methodological and ethical problems posed by interviewing people with developmental disabilities—using standard interview methods, at least—seem to argue for proxy interviews.

In the case of people with developmental disabilities, however, the quality of proxy data may be affected in a number of ways. For example, the accuracy of data gathered may vary depending on the relationship with the subject. A proxy who is a live-in relative of a respondent will presumably be better able to provide accurate information than a more distant acquaintance. Still, the ability to respond accurately does not guarantee that genuine responses will be provided. For instance, the accuracy of data is jeopardized when assessing the victimization of a person whose proxy interview is conducted with the person who is the perpetrator.

The NCVS allows respondents to be interviewed by proxy (usually another member of the household) if the respondent is a minor child, away for the entire interview period, or physically or mentally incapacitated; incapacitation can range from hearing impairment to severe mental retardation.

In 1997, approximately 4 percent of all NCVS personal victimization interviews were conducted by proxy. Of these, 30 percent were justified by physical or mental incapacity. Just 37 victimization incidents were reported by proxies, suggesting that mentally or physically incapacitated people faced significantly lower risks of victimization than the general population (see Table 4-1). If specific crimes are examined, however, mentally or physically incapacitated persons had a significantly higher risk of sexual assault—they were nearly twice as likely to report (by proxy) a sexual assault. The higher risk of sexual assault is consistent with the findings of Wilson and Brewer (see Table 4-2) and with the prevailing theory of victimization. The lower risks of assault and robbery may be an artifact of the proxy interview method or differences in the sample. In addition, people with disabilities

TABLE 4-1 Proxy Victimization Risks for Persons with Disabilities Relative to the General Population

Crime	Number of Victims	Relative Risk
Any	37	0.13
Sexual assault	4	1.95
Burglary	2	0.76
Assault	4	0.14
Robbery	11	0.21
Auto theft	0	NA
Theft	18	0.10
Other theft	2	0.17
All other crimes	10	0.13

SOURCE: Data from 1997 National Crime Victimization Survey, v3046, v3040, v3034, v3036, v3038, v3042, v3044, v3048.

TABLE 4-2 Victimization Risk by Intellectual Disability

	Intellectually Disabled		
Crime	Yes	No	Relative Risk
Assault	11.4	4.0	2.8
Sexual assault	3.2	0.3	10.7
Robbery	5.1	0.4	12.8
Total personal	19.7	4.7	4.2
Auto theft	0.6	0.7	0.9
Theft	7.6	6.4	1.2
Burglary	11.4	6.4	1.8
Household theft	4.4	3.7	1.2
Total property	24.0	17.2	1.4

SOURCE: Data from Wilson and Brewer (1992).

may be at lower risk for such crimes as theft and robbery if their mobility is restricted and they spend limited time in public places.

Proxy interview data are also widely used in clinical practice and research on elderly patients with senile dementia. In these types of interviews, the elderly patient is too cognitively impaired to respond to standard neuropsychological test items, so the caregiver—usually an adult child or spouse—gives proxy responses. A 1995 study conducted by researchers from the UCI Alzheimer's Disease Center (McCleary et al., 1996b) brings the validity of proxy interviews into question.

In a subset of this study (McCleary et al., 1996a), 81 percent of caretakers for 221 elderly demented patients were adult children of the patients—who were roughly similar to caretakers of persons with developmental disabilities. Three events—injury, aggression, and loss of a functional activity—were examined. Researchers found that these events were grossly underreported by the caretaker proxy. The actual annualized incidence rate of injury, for example, was more than five times higher than the rate reported by the caretakers.

Communication Barriers

The validity of survey responses depends on the subject's ability to understand the question and whether the subject comprehends what is a criminal event. But some people who have been victimized, such as those who are young or developmentally disabled, may not even recognize that the event was inappropriate or illegal. In addition, because there are no published studies like that of Goodman, Toby, Batterman-Faunce, Orcutt, Sherry, Shapiro, and Sachsenmaier (1998) on children's recall of traumatic events, little is known about the ability of people with a developmental disability to recall stressful events accurately. On this issue, McCleary and Wiebe could only describe unpublished research conducted for the Arc of the United States to suggest that the NCVS may not be adequate for assessing self-reported victimization among respondents with developmental disabilities.

SURVEYING THE INSTITUTIONAL SUBPOPULATION

A large proportion of people with developmental disabilities resides in nursing homes, halfway houses, hospitals, and jails and prisons. As stated above, because NCVS interviews are conducted by households, this population is automatically excluded from the sample data.

With the exception of the Bureau of Justice Statistics' annual Survey of Inmates in Local Jails, few surveys are designed to adequately assess institutional risk, especially in cases in which a large proportion of the subpopulation of interest may reside in institutions instead of households.

The 1996 survey, which was based on in-person interviews with a national representative sample of 573,000 inmates in U.S. jails, identified inmates with disabilities as people who were having difficulty seeing regular newsprint (even with glasses), difficulty hearing normal conversation (even with a hearing aid), a mental or emotional condition, a learning disability, speech impediment, or physical or emotional condition that limited work. The survey found that, in general, inmates with a learning disability, difficulty seeing, a physical or mental condition that limits work, or a mental or emotional condition, were at higher risk for violence and that those with a mental or emotional condition were at significantly higher risk (Harlow, 1998). When these data were reanalyzed and demographic, criminological, and contextual confounds were controlled for, however, the risks for inmates who reported a mental or emotional condition were found to be insignificant. These new findings illustrate three types of problems with the initial survey: (1) screening biases that led to significant numbers of false positives in the disability categories (because these nondisabled inmates face lower risks, their experiences bias the relative risk toward zero); (2) conventional survey interviewing methods are not appropriate here; institutional pressures on victims create an incentive to misreport; and (3) vagueness of the disability item limits the utility of the data.

Better Survey Design

Based on their review of the problem and the literature, McCleary and Wiebe conclude that no existing survey can be adapted to provide estimates of disability-specific victimization. They noted that valid estimation of disability-specific victimization requires instead a sample survey designed specifically for that purpose. They provide specific guidance on such a survey's sample design, indicating that it should tap both the institutional and noninstitutional subpopulations, tap the proportion of the population that is moving between the institutional and noninstitutional subpopulations, and be sufficiently large to ensure nominal power for contrasts with the population of people without disabilities. Furthermore, McCleary and Wiebe note that the survey's interview methods must use items designed specifically for the subpopulation with developmental disabilities, use proxy responses only as a last resort, and use interview prompts in a manner guaranteed to produce responses of known validity.

Bureau of Justice Statistics Action Plan

Despite the difficulties noted above, the Crime Victims with Disabilities Awareness Act of 1998 requires the Bureau of Justice Statistics to collect data under the NCVS. In response, BJS has conducted its own review of the literature cited in this report and has undertaken a number of activities to address the law's mandate. These include meeting with national and state officials working in the area of disability and becoming active participants in two working groups dealing with disability statistics: a government-wide group, the Federal Interagency Subcommittee on Disability Statistics (ISDS), which meets on a monthly basis to discuss the issues related to identifying people with disabilities and coordinate research in this area; and a research group convened by the Bureau of Labor Statistics to help design questions related to disability on the Current Population Survey (CPS). BJS has also established relationships with people in the disability research and advocacy communities in order to ensure that its efforts would be accepted as true reflections of the victimization experiences of people with disabilities.

In August 1999, BJS convened a group of experts from inside and outside the federal government to begin the coordination process, obtain information about other disability-related surveys, and brainstorm on the issues and possible strategies. In October 1999, BJS officials participated in the workshop that is summarized in this report. Based on all of these activities and a review of the attributes of the NCVS, BJS staff began to construct a strategy, the components of which are:

1. Adding questions to the existing NCVS to determine whether a person has a disability.
2. Developing modifications to question wordings, proxy respondent rules, interview procedures, and interviewer training to improve the information-gathering process in the context of the NCVS interview.
3. Exploring enhancement of the NCVS sampling frame to oversample people with disabilities.
4. Exploring enhancement of the NCVS sampling frame to include an institutional component.

Given the difficulties, detailed in this chapter, of using the NCVS to measure the victimization of people with disabilities, this strategy is being implemented in phases. The first two items constitute the first phase and are the focus of current efforts. The last two items have been discussed but are presently tabled as future activities until BJS can determine whether the first phase can be completed successfully.[1]

---

[1] The material on current and future BJS plans is briefly summarized here from a paper entitled "Developing the Capability to Measure Crime Victimization of People With Disabilities," delivered at the 2000 National Conference of the American Society of Criminology in San Francisco, November 17, 2000, by Michael Rand, Victimization Statistics, Bureau of Justice Statistics.

5

Criminal Justice System Responses

In the last approximately 25 years, American society has made significant advances in providing support to people with developmental disabilities in the efforts of these individuals to achieve fair treatment. Major societal institutions, including education, business, and medicine, have responded to create fairer and less discriminatory treatment for all people with disabilities. However, not all societal institutions have responded with the same speed or thoughtfulness. We can quibble about whether education or medicine responded more quickly to the societal need to end discrimination, or even whether either institution has fully succeeded. But I don't think there is much question that of all societal institutions, the criminal justice system is the last to adequately respond to the special circumstances of people with developmental disabilities. This remains true whether the individual with a disability has been accused of committing a crime or is the victim of crime. For people with developmental disabilities, the criminal justice system is the last frontier of integration.

Ruth Luckasson, Workshop Presenter

Many people with developmental disabilities are ill-equipped to cope with the criminal justice system. Very little research exists on their interaction with the police or the courts. In an effort to address how the justice system currently responds to crimes against the developmentally disabled, and how that response can be improved, the workshop therefore concentrated on ways in which laws and legal practice concerning competence and consent may act as a barrier to involvement in the legal process of crime victims with developmental disabilities and the ways in which laws, such as the Americans with Disabilities Act and hate crime legislation, may serve to overcome some of those barriers. This chapter examines these three responses of the law and the criminal justice system to people with disabilities. First, drawing on the paper by Robert Dinerstein, it examines the legal issues of consent, capacity, and accommodations as they affect people with disabilities. Second, drawing on the paper by Leigh Ann Davis, it considers how accommodations required by the Americans with Disabilities Act can be used to assist people with disabilities. Third, drawing on the paper by Ryken Grattet and Valerie Jenness, it explores the viability of using hate crime law to protect people with disabilities.

PARTICIPATION IN THE CRIMINAL JUSTICE SYSTEM

People with mental retardation may be defendants in criminal cases, charged with crimes that range from simple misdemeanors to serious felonies that can subject them to life sentences without parole or even the death penalty. They may be witnesses to crimes allegedly committed by defendants against others. They may be victims of crimes committed against themselves, with the crimes ranging from simple misdemeanor theft—for example, someone stealing an article of their clothing—to more serious crimes, such as sexual assault and rape. They may participate as jurors, judging the conduct of others charged with crimes. They may participate in civil cases in ways that are analogous to those delineated above in criminal cases. These forms of participation occur in the courts of all 50 states and the District of Columbia, and, to a lesser extent, in federal courts as well.

Dinerstein identifies basic principles that underlie the capacity (often called competency) of people with developmental disabilities to participate in and consent to various decisions as victims and witnesses in court proceedings.

Capacity and Consent

Historically, society often assumed that people with disabilities—especially those with cognitive disabilities such as mental retardation—were not competent to express their preferences or give consent. Many people with disabilities in fact may not have the functional capacity to consent to various actions. But the lack of capacity often has less to do with a person's inherent limitations than with societal attitudes that limit opportunities for people to make choices and to receive guidance and training in making those choices wisely.

Capacity is not an all-or-nothing proposition. Individuals, including those with disabilities, can have capacity in some areas and lack it in others (Luckasson et al., 1992). Thus, for example, demonstrating that a woman has the capacity to enter into marriage and consent to the adoption of a child does not necessarily imply that she is capable of consenting to sexual relations with someone not her husband (see, for example, *State v. Soura*, 796 P. 2d 109, Idaho, 1990).

Nevertheless, as a matter of law, it has long been true that people with disabilities are presumed to be competent (or have capacity) unless proven otherwise. This presumption, which also applies to witness testimony in court cases, has important implications for people with disabilities and their meaningful participation in society. Among other things, it means that a person with disabilities is entitled to full participation on equal terms with others. A statute or practice that as a general matter prevents all people with mental retardation from testifying in court, for example, would violate this principle of presumed capacity (see, for example, *State v. Henderson*, 607 So. 2d 733, La. Ct. App., 1992).

Capacity, which may be thought of as a person's inherent ability to make a rational decision or give meaningful consent (Stefan, 1996), is only one element of the consent equation. In addition, an individual must have sufficient information to give consent, and the consent must be given voluntarily (Appelbaum and Grisso, 1995; Ellis, 1992). Consent, and its co-relative concept, choice, do not exist in a vacuum. While freedom to choose and give consent are important values for people with developmental disabilities, they must sometimes be balanced against protecting them from exploitation, abuse, and other forms of harm.

Participation in Court Proceedings

The presumption of capacity applies in many court jurisdictions. For example, in the federal system, Federal Rule of Evidence 601 provides that "every person is competent to be a witness" unless proven otherwise. Many state evidence rules follow the federal rule and likewise presume the competence of all witnesses (Sobsey, 1994).

When there is cause to question a person's competence as a witness—which could be for reasons other than the person's disability or age (such as lacking personal knowledge of the event in question)—the court can hold a preliminary hearing outside the earshot of the jury to determine if the person is competent to testify. Determining if a witness or victim is competent to testify does not mean that the testimony will necessarily be believed. It is for the trier of fact—usually a jury but possibly a judge—to determine if the witness's testimony is credible. But it may not always be possible for the trier of fact to understand the extent to which the witness's disability may affect the manner as well as the substance of the person's testimony. In such cases, it may be appropriate for the proponent of the testimony, or the court itself, to call an expert witness to explain the context (although it would be inappropriate for the expert to opine whether the witness's testimony is true) (see, for example, *People v. Herring*, 20 Cal. App. 4th 1066, Ct. App, 1993).

Capacity and consent play an important part in another aspect of the criminal justice system that is particularly relevant to people with developmental disabilities who are victims of sexual assault and abuse. Every state's rape law criminalizes sexual intercourse with a woman who lacks capacity or is unable to give consent (Denno, 1997; Larsen, 1992). At first glance, it might seem inconsistent to prosecute someone on the basis of a victim's lack of capacity to consent to sex, and then to permit the victim to testify to the events in question, which is necessarily dependent on her capacity to be a witness (see *State v. Gonsalves*, 706 P. 2d 659, 662, Haw. Ct. Apps., 1985). But the inconsistency is more apparent than real. State statutes typically define sexual offenses aggravated by the victim's incapacity as those based on her inability to understand the nature of the sexual conduct or appraise its consequences (Denno, 1997). This test presupposes the victim's inability to understand the moral and societal elements of the act as well as its possible medical consequences; it requires the victim to be able to engage in abstract thought (*State v. Gonsalves*). The test for witness competence, as noted above, focuses more on the accuracy of perceptions, the ability to communicate, and an understanding of the obligation to tell the truth. With the possible exception of the truth-telling obligation, these elements are decidedly more concrete than the ability to appraise consequences. The truth-telling obligation, even if somewhat abstract, entails a less complex thought process and is less dependent on social and community knowledge than is appraising the social meaning of sexual intercourse.

Enhancing the Capacity of Victims Within the Court System

Before Coming to Court

Enhancing the capacity of people with developmental disabilities to report crimes requires that agencies, family members, and advocates develop support mechanisms for them, according to Dinerstein. These supports can be as basic as providing an advocate who has had some training in criminal justice issues to assist the victim in understanding how the process works. The advocate also can serve as an important liaison between the person with a disability and police investigators. In this respect, the advocate can play a critical role in urging the police to vary their questioning techniques to increase the accuracy of the information the victim provides and to take the crime report seriously.

For example, the suggestibility and willingness to please of some persons with developmental disabilities counsel against some police investigatory techniques that might lead to unintentionally false testimony from the witness. Having an advocate assist the person with disabilities navigate through the criminal justice system is important, but agencies and caregivers can help by taking proactive measures to educate their clients about the criminal justice system before they become involved with it.

It is important for advocates, family members, and others who may assist victims with disabilities to remember that it is the person with a disability who is the victim, not them. Oftentimes, witnesses without disabilities choose not to pursue criminal complaints. Sometimes their reasons are quite understandable; other times, they may be the product of real or imagined coercion from others. These same considerations apply for people with disabilities. The advocate or family member can counsel the client or loved one on the advantages and disadvantages of pursuing a complaint, and take steps to ensure that the decision to proceed (or to decline to do so) is truly the decision of the victim.

Participation Once the Matter Becomes a Court Case

The advocate for the victim with disabilities can play an important role in serving as a middle person between the prosecutor's office and the victim. While prosecution offices increasingly employ people as victim and witness coordinators, these staff members may or may not be knowledgeable about people with disabilities. The advocate for the victim, at a minimum, can ensure that the prosecution office's coordinator is kept apprised of the needs of the victim for more information, provided in a nontechnical manner, than a witness without disabilities may require.

Florida, for example, requires the court to appoint an advocate for a victim or witness with mental retardation in abuse and neglect and sexual offense cases, and it permits such an appointment in any other criminal case. The advocate is empowered to represent the person in all court proceedings; must have access to all evidence and receive copies of reports introduced in the case; must receive notice of court proceedings; and may interview witnesses and request additional examinations by doctors, psychiatrists, or psychologists.

Advocates can help demystify the court process for the witness with developmental disabilities by having the person observe a court proceeding in advance of the one in which the person will be involved. The advocate would accompany the person to the proceeding and be available to explain the proceedings during and after the fact.

Testimony in Court

Once a trial begins, the focus will be on the testimony of the victim or witness with disabilities. As noted previously, most courts presume the competence of witnesses, although they may conduct a preliminary hearing to assure themselves that the person with developmental disabilities in fact has the capacity to testify. While the person's direct testimony is the preferred method of presenting evidence, indirect methods, including reports from people to whom the victim or witness confided or expert testimony regarding the effect of developmental disabilities, may also be admissible as adjuncts to, or in lieu of, the person's testimony. Courts also may be inclined to permit the witness with developmental disabilities to testify on videotape or otherwise out of the presence of the defendant (or in his presence but in a less intimidating atmosphere than a courtroom), although such substitutes for direct testimony may have a significant impact on a defendant's Sixth Amendment right to confront the witnesses against him.

These and other accommodations to the witness with mental retardation, as well as many others that could be described, not only represent good policy and practice, but also are required by Title II of the Americans with Disabilities Act and its accompanying regulations (28 CFR § 35.104 et seq.). But any accommodations must be provided in as nondiscriminatory and integrated a way as possible (28 CFR § 35.130(d)), so that if there were two possible accommodations available, the court would be bound to choose the one that permitted the witness to testify most closely to the ways others do.

After the Trial

Witnesses and victims increasingly have the right to participate in sentencing hearings held for convicted defendants. Indeed, in some circumstances, a victim can present testimony, directly or indirectly, at such a hearing even if she did not testify at the trial (and, of course, could do so if there was no trial but rather a plea agreement). The advocate's role discussed in the pretrial context is fully applicable after trial as well. The advocate's role is to continue to explain the nature of the proceeding to the person with developmental disabilities, assisting the person, if necessary, in presenting oral or written testimony of the effect of the crime on him or her, and otherwise continue explaining the proceedings and reinforcing the person's understanding of them. Once the defendant is sentenced, the victim may also need to be kept informed of such things as parole eligibility dates, although the advocate should be sensitive to the person's desire not to have such information if that is the person's choice, and if consistent with his or her safety.

THE AMERICANS WITH DISABILITIES ACT

The Americans with Disabilities Act (ADA), signed into law on July 26, 1990, bans discrimination based on having a disability. It provides people with developmental disabilities the civil rights protections similar to the rights provided on the basis of race, sex, national origin, and religion. It guarantees equal opportunity for people with developmental disabilities in employment, public accommodations, transportation, state and local government services, and telecommunication relay services. Title II of the ADA specifically prohibits state and local governments from discriminating against an individual with a disability. State and local government services include police, court, and corrections systems.

The ADA has improved the response of the criminal justice system to people with disabilities in a number of ways since 1990. Courts must make reasonable accommodations for people with disabilities upon request, unless such accommodation fundamentally alters its activity or structure or involves an undue financial burden. Accommodations are now being used in classrooms, in court testimony, and in some instances in interrogations. Some courts do provide disability advocates to assist with criminal cases involving people with disabilities, although this appears to be rare. The ADA has also been useful in creating and disseminating information to educate law enforcement professionals, although this continues to be a major need.

The police have typically been the focus of attention with regard to training on disability issues, but other equally important professions remain in need of education. The victim assistance field has not identified the best practices for serving victims with unique needs, nor has it learned the most effective way to train the criminal justice community about assisting victims with developmental disabilities (Tyiska, 1998).

Law Enforcement Training

In a study of police officers' training on disability issues, McAfee and Musso (1995) found that the only disability receiving notable attention in police literature is mental illness. Their state-by-state analysis revealed that only four states had training on mental retardation, two states had training on developmental disabilities, and one included learning disabilities (McAfee and Musso, 1995). It is not surprising, then, that officers believe stereotypes about people with developmental disabilities as fact. Sobsey (1994) describes five areas that should be incorporated into the ideal police training on people with disabilities: attitude training; awareness of medical and legal needs; multidisciplinary teamwork—learning how to coordinate with other agency staff who work with this population; court orientation—recognizing the complexity involved in bringing a victim to court; and specialist versus generalist training, in which some officers are given more detailed training to act as consultants in cases involving people with disabilities.

The Arc of the United States has created a curriculum entitled "Understanding Mental Retardation: Training for Law Enforcement." Designed to take about three hours, it includes a video, worksheets, and handouts. The training covers such areas as understanding and identifying people with mental retardation, understanding different mental retardation syndromes, including fetal alcohol syndrome, fragile X, and Down syndrome, and understanding other disabilities, such as cerebral palsy, epilepsy, deafness, Tourette's syndrome, and mental illness (see http://thearc.org/ada/crim.html). In addition, the training helps to create greater police awareness of the prevalence of victimization among people with developmental disabilities by including a section on why they are more likely to be victimized.

Critical Focus, a California training corporation, has produced a telecourse entitled "Law Enforcement Response to Persons with Developmental Disabilities," which has been certified by the State of California's Peace Officer Standards and Training Commission. This course specifically focuses on people with developmental disabilities and is designed to give law enforcement and correctional officers an understanding of what developmental disabilities are and what techniques are the best in responding to this population. The training teaches officers how to recognize an individual with different developmental disabilities, how to communicate with them, and in the event of arrest or victimization, how to modify interview procedures. The disabilities covered include mental retardation, cerebral palsy, epilepsy, traumatic brain injury, and autism. Critical Focus also has a "Train the Trainers" course that teaches officers how to train other officers within their department about interacting with people with developmental disabilities. In addition to training, a few police departments are developing "crisis intervention teams" to deal with people with developmental disabilities. For example, the Seattle Police Department is starting to train detectives to work on cases involving domestic violence and sexual assault of victims with disabilities.

Overall, however, such efforts on the part of law enforcement are uncommon. The Davis paper concluded that certain changes can be made immediately that do not create undue hardship, and police can continue to learn about developmental disabilities in the process. She observed that waiting until the law enforcement profession learns more about developmental disabilities should not become an excuse for not taking action and implementing practical accommodations.

Improving Reporting Rates

As discussed in earlier chapters, there are many reasons why offenses against people with disabilities go unreported. According to Davis, most rape crisis centers do not have staff members who know about developmental disabilities and may never even recognize that a person needs accommodation. Some victim assistance centers may be overwhelmed by the needs of this population and are not trained how to assist victims with disabilities.

Another obstacle to reporting is the victim's fear of not being believed or taken seriously. According to several reports (Hickman, 1998; Roeher Institute, 1994; Sanders et al., 1997), women with disabilities often have negative experiences with police officers, which makes it unlikely they will pursue future contact with them. The reports suggest that many of the attitudes, stereotypes, and myths held by the public regarding women with disabilities are also prevalent among members of the police force. Police believe victims with disabilities lack credibility and, in addition, the police themselves lack standardized protocols for handling complaints by victims with disabilities, so that responses are often individualized by the first responder (Roeher Institute, 1994; Sanders et al., 1997).

For example, Hickman (1998) reports that if a woman who has a speech impairment calls the police, she may "sound incoherent and rambling. . . . [T]hey think you're drunk and just dismiss you." This assertion is backed up by another report stating that officers' negative attitudes about people who have trouble communicating may impede the investigation (Roeher Institute, 1994), and one report from England stating that if "a person is not able to communicate well, the police officer may see this as grounds for not pursuing a complaint" (Sanders et al., 1997).

Some states have attempted to improve the rate of reporting by enacting legislation. For example, Connecticut passed legislation in 1985 making it mandatory to report suspected abuse of adults with mental retardation. Although such laws can help educate others about victimization among people with developmental disabilities, Davis suggested, they hold little power if attitudinal barriers are not addressed by building significant, ongoing collaborations among the systems involved.

HATE CRIME LAW

Given the problems regarding the shortcomings in the criminal justice response to people with developmental disabilities, proposals for reforms have been itemized and articulated by the Office of Victims of Crime in a bulletin on "Working with Victims of Crime with Disabilities" (Tyiska, 1998). Sponsored by the U.S. Department of Justice, this publication makes specific policy recommendations, including increasing the accessibility of the criminal justice system through everything from architectural changes to the introduction of communication technologies; creating training measures for sensitizing law enforcement officials to the needs of people with disabilities; fostering relations with disability service and advocacy organizations in the community; improving data collection efforts; and introducing specific protocols to assist people with disabilities in the criminal justice process and to protect them from retaliation.

Writing for the Office for Victims of Crime, Tyiska recommended that hate crime law be applied to crimes against people with disabilities, specifically that "prosecutors should invoke hate crime statutes, if indicated, when prosecuting crimes against people with disabilities. Judges should apply equal sentencing or sentencing enhancements, when allowed, for offenders who victimize people with disabilities" (Tyiska, 1998:4). Notably, a critical discussion of the relationship between crimes against people with disabilities and the parameters of hate crime—as a social behavior and a recently developed corpus of law—has yet to develop. Several workshop participants therefore described the principles underlying hate crime statutes and then explored the connections between hate crimes and people with disabilities.

Criminalization of Discriminatory Violence

In the late 1970s and early 1980s, lawmakers throughout the United States began to respond to what they perceived to be an escalation of violence directed at minorities with a novel legal strategy: the criminalization of discriminatory violence, now commonly referred to as "hate crime." Throughout the late 1980s and into the 1990s, most state legislatures passed at least one piece of hate crime legislation; the federal government also passed three hate crime laws (Jacobs and Potter, 1998; Jenness, 1999; Jenness and Grattet, 1996, 2000; Grattet et al., 1998; Soule and Earl, 1999). The general rationale for this legislation has been that harassment and intimidation, assault, destruction of property, and other forms of violent crime assume a particularly dangerous and socially disruptive character when motivated by bigotry and manifested as discrimination.

It is useful to ask two interrelated questions about hate crime law and its relationship to people with developmental disabilities. First, to what degree have state and federal policy makers recognized them as a constituency particularly vulnerable to discriminatory violence and thus worthy of recognition in hate crime law? Second, on what basis should specific constituencies, such as people with disabilities, be considered for inclusion in hate crime law?

The most direct way to answer the first question is to examine the status provisions (Jenness and Grattet, 2000) or what others have referred to as "target groups" (Soule and Earl, 1999) referenced in state hate crime law. In 1988, the most common status provisions were for race, religion, color, and national origin. This represents a legal response to the most visible, recognizable, and stereotypical kinds of discriminatory behavior (Levin and McDevitt, 1993). Disability was included in only 5 of the 19 states that had passed laws by 1988. By 1998, however, a second tier of categories clearly emerged, with sexual orientation, gender, and disabilities becoming increasingly recognized in state hate crime law.

Following the states' lead, Congress passed three laws specifically designed to address bias-motivated violence, and it continues to debate additional legislation. In 1990, President Bush signed the Hate Crimes Statistics Act (PL 101-275), which requires the U.S. attorney general to collect statistical data on "crimes that manifest evidence of prejudice based on race, religion, sexual orientation, or ethnicity, including where appropriate the crimes of murder, nonnegligent manslaughter, forcible rape; aggravated assault, simple assault, intimidation; arson; and destruction, damage or vandalism of property."

In 1994, Congress passed two more hate crime laws. The Violence Against Women Act (PL 103-322) specifies that "all persons within the United States shall have the right to be free from crimes of violence motivated by gender." The Hate Crimes Sentencing Enhancement Act (PL 103-322) identifies eight crimes—murder; non-negligent manslaughter; forcible rape; aggravated assault; simple assaults; intimidation; arson; and destruction, damage, or vandalism of property—for which judges are allowed to enhance penalties.

As both the federal and state laws reveal, addressing crimes against people with disabilities has found a strategy in hate crime legislation, albeit rather late in the lawmaking process. Indeed, although disability is included formally in many state and the federal laws, its later entry into the laws has meant that its connection to the legal and conceptual definition of hate crime remains rather tenuous. Only half the states have laws that cover disability. Data collection efforts continue to lag behind other groups. Police training publications and curriculum at federal, state, and local levels tend to discuss disability-based hate crime only infrequently, if at all (Jenness and Grattet, 2000). There have been no appellate cases dealing with the disability provision, so that the special problems it might present have not been analyzed (Phillips and Grattet, 1999). Thus, as both a legislative provision and practical issue, disability remains less embedded in the law than the race, religion, ethnicity, sexual orientation, and gender provisions.

Although people with disabilities remain less visible as victims of hate crime than the other minority groups included in the laws (e.g., blacks, Jews, immigrants), they are still more visible than other groups that have been proposed (e.g., union members, the elderly, children, police officers). A comparison along these lines raises the question: On what criteria should selection for inclusion in hate crime law proceed? Why some and not others?

Key Criteria for Inclusion

For a group to be recognized, hate crime law requires that it be seen by some portion of society as an identifiable group of persons who, to some degree, maintain a collective identity (Taylor and Whittier, 1992). Two sources of evidence suggest that people with disabilities comprise a "self-regarding group." First, survey data suggest that persons with disabilities do, indeed, feel a common identity with one another and see themselves as a minority in the same sense as people who are black or Hispanic (Hill et al., 1986). Second, people with disabilities have, over the past two decades, emerged to become a significant sector of the modern civil rights movement (Shapiro, 1993). Much like people of color, gays and lesbians, and women, people with disabilities constitute an identifiable sector of a larger civil rights movement in the United States (Shapiro, 1993).

Every self-regarding group, however, is not an equally viable contender for inclusion in hate crime law. Rather, those constituencies sharing a characteristic that implicates deep social divisions are prime candidates (Lawrence, 1999). Historians, criminologists, activists, and various state agencies have only recently begun to document the influence of disability as a predisposing factor in discriminatory violence. With the passage of the ADA in 1990, the federal government recognized "that disabled persons have been subject to a history of purposeful unequal treatment . . . in our society."

According to Grattet and Jenness, research suggests that the visibility of violence against people with disabilities has reached the point at which the visibility of violence directed at people of color and gays and lesbians was not so long ago. Moreover, they noted that violence is being increasingly understood as central to the subordination of persons with disabilities.

Hate Crime Motivations

Symbolic crimes are best envisioned as social crimes, because the victim is selected precisely because of what he or she symbolizes. In contrast, actuarial crimes involve the selection of a victim based on his or her real or imagined social characteristic, but not for expressive or symbolic reasons.

Related to the distinction between symbolic and actuarial crimes, a distinction can be made between what are called the discriminatory selection model and the racial animus model (Lawrence, 1999). The discriminatory selection model defines hate crime solely on the basis of the perpetrator's discriminatory selection of a victim, regardless of why such a selection was made. For example, like girls and women, people with disabilities may be targeted simply because they are perceived to be more vulnerable victims. In sharp contrast, the racial animus model focuses attention on the reason for discriminatory selection of victims. This approach assumes that the motivation for the selection of a victim is less instrumental and more expressive; perpetrators use the act of victimization to express animus toward the category of persons the victim represents (e.g., a person of color, a homosexual, a Jew, a person with a disability).

Both the discriminatory selection model and the racial animus model can be applied to the circumstances of violence against people with disabilities. Some evidence suggests that persons with disabilities face higher rates of victimization, not because perpetrators harbor ill will toward them, but because they are in vulnerable situations.

Since the invention of the term "hate crime" in the late 1970s, lawmakers and judges have increasingly agreed that the parameters of the discriminatory selection model provide the most legitimate foundation for modern hate crime law. Early in the history of lawmaking around hate crime, lawmakers experimented with ways of phrasing the intent standard as they grappled with how to write hate crime law. The emergent legitimate form of the law does not distinguish between mere bias-intent and hatred. Similarly, appellate court decisions on hate crime cases have, over time, increasingly endorsed the "because of" phrasing in hate crime law. In so doing, courts have maintained that it does not matter what political views or ideologies motivated the act. All that matters is that a victim was selected "because of" their race, religion, national origin etc., quite apart from the degree of malice involved on the part of the perpetrator (Phillips and Grattet, 1999). This has caused some to shift from using the term "hate" crime to the term "bias" crime. Presumably, the same logic would apply to violence directed at people with disabilities. These trends in law-making and judicial decision making suggest that the least stringent form of motivational phrasing, which maps onto the discriminatory selection model, is increasingly dominant.

Implications

Hate crime laws treat people with disabilities as both "different from" and "the same as" other people by simultaneously segregating and integrating them from or into the criminal justice system. Envisioning crimes against people with disabilities as hate crimes entails according special treatment to them. This is accomplished by extending the "same" treatment accorded to other similarly situated groups. With regard to the difference dimension, when applied to persons with disabilities, hate crime law bestows minority status on 54 million people with disabilities in the United States (U.S. Census Bureau, 1997), thus distinguishing them from the rest of the U.S. population. With regard to sameness, the institutionalization of disability provisions in hate crime law serves to include people with disabilities into the coalition of status groups already covered under the law, ensuring there is nothing special or different about them.

Grattet and Jenness note that not all crimes against people with disabilities should be conceived of as hate crimes. Just as this approach would not be appropriate for other categories such as race, religion, sexual orientation, and gender, it would not be appropriate for disabilities. As with other sorts of bias crimes, enhancements should be reserved for instances in which there is persuasive evidence that the selection of the victim was based, in whole or in part, on the victim's disability.

SUMMARY

There are a number of barriers to the participation in the criminal justice system of crime victims with developmental disabilities. Police and prosecutors may see them as unreliable witnesses and be reluctant to bring charges when the victim has a developmental disability. People with developmental disabilities may require support, such as a specialized advocate, to assist them in dealing with the criminal justice system, from dealing with the police investigating the crime through the entire court process. The Americans with Disabilities Act, in fact, requires accommodations to meet the needs of people with disabilities. The criminal justice system has begun to make changes to accommodate the needs of people with disabilities, but much remains to be done in the areas of training law enforcement and court personnel and in providing advocates and other resources to people with disabilities.

An area of law that is emerging as another avenue to better include victims with disabilities in the criminal justice system is hate crime legislation. Although some states have included disability as one of the groups in their hate crime laws, few cases have made use of it, so that special problems it may present have yet to be analyzed.

Research is sparse on the effects of accommodations required by the Americans with Disabilities Act and inclusion of disability in hate crime legislation. It remains to be known how well these approaches will be able to overcome the barriers to participation by victims with disabilities in the criminal justice system.

6

Treatment Issues

As this report notes, almost no research exists on the impact of victimization on people with developmental disabilities or on the type of treatment or programs that would be most helpful to them. In an effort to examine the social service system response to crime victims with disabilities and how that response can be improved, the National Research Council asked Nora Baladerian, a clinician with extensive experience in treating persons with disabilities, to write a paper on these issues. This chapter is based on that paper, which was drawn from her clinical experience. Baladerian views the lack of research on these matters as a barrier both to preventing victimization of persons with developmental disabilities and to improving services for them.

Victimization may affect people with developmental disabilities at least as powerfully as the rest of the population, and perhaps more so. Because of a lack of preparation, information, education, and support, it is likely that in an assault, confusion may heighten terror, and may cause greater levels of distrust, depression, anxiety, and the other well-recognized responses to trauma among people with disabilities. The personal impact of maltreatment for a child or adult crime victim may depend on any of several important factors: the role of the perpetrator vis-à-vis the victim; the number of attacks; the response of the family and others to warning of the attack; and the time and choice for future activities allowed the victim. Because the perpetrator is most likely to be someone in a position of trust or perhaps of love with the victim with a disability, the closer the relationship, the more devastating the impact of the abuse. Betrayal can lead to an inability to regain trust, including trust of oneself.

Both in child abuse and sexual assault, the response of others upon learning of the assault has been identified as a critical factor in healing the victim. When the family and others close to the victim have a negative reaction, blame the victim, do not want to ever talk about what happened, do not believe that it happened, or protect the perpetrator, the results are psychologically devastating and set up a poor prognosis for the victim's ability to heal from the trauma. How the case is handled by the law enforcement agencies also has a powerful impact on the victim.

How victimization affects an individual may depend on these significant factors:

- If the victim feels responsible for the crime or participation in the crime;
- If, prior to the attack, the victim had poor self-regard as a chronic or temporary state of mind;
- If the immediate response to the learning of the attack is empowering and supporting; and
- If she is informed that many women become victims of assault and that this did not happen because of who she is, but because the perpetrator is a person of bad intentions and a criminal.

In assessing a crime victim for adjudication or mental health treatment, an understanding of these factors is critical. The individual's self-image and sense of empowerment or dependence will affect her experience and self-explanation of the crime. Rape trauma syndrome and post-traumatic stress disorder (PTSD) are well recognized as encompassing the range of normal psychological responses to trauma. Victims of sexual assault have more intense and perhaps more frequent physical reactions than those of victims of other types of crime. Physical changes that are obvious are changes in eating and sleeping routines, mood changes, and an overall level of more neediness (for children, a reversion to an earlier stage of life that required great nurturing and attention). In addition, crime victims may run away; stop eating altogether; eat only certain foods or a certain type or consistency of food; refuse to change clothes, bathe, or wash hair; cut hair; become aggressive or sexualized; begin sexual self-stimulation or mutilation; acquire or request change in hair color, tattooing, piercing, type of clothing; reenact the crime; or become extremely overweight or dangerously underweight.

The family will most likely become secondary trauma victims, exhibiting similar responses as described in PTSD, including depression, anxiety, rage, denial, and reliving the event based on what they have learned. Changes in the victim's personality can be expected, usually for the worse. The individual can be expected to withdraw socially, become irritable, and perhaps initiate the use of profanity or sexually related words or phrases. She can become obstinate, stubborn, demanding, or noncompliant and have a "don't care" attitude. Or she may simply withdraw and refuse to speak to anyone or participate in any social activity.

TECHNIQUES THAT HELP ABUSE AND CRIME VICTIMS

Psychological treatment and psychiatric treatment are important to the healing process for any victim, according to Baladerian, and thus for the crime victim with a disability. In many cases, no qualified practitioner is available for either individual or group treatment for victims with disabilities. Involvement of the family members in the treatment is a critical aspect to working with crime victims with developmental disabilities. Baladerian indicated that very few mental health practitioners demonstrate an interest in treating crime victims with a disability and that an exploration into motivating interest in such treatment is needed.

Why mental health providers do not acquire training in this specialty may be a function of the general societal lack of interest in people with disabilities, Baladerian noted. Most people agree that the majority of people involved with disability issues, regardless of the field of endeavor, have taken an interest because of a personal experience. Psychologists or other mental health practitioners who graduate from any college today are likely to have received one hour or less of training on treating people with disabilities.

SERVICES FOR CRIME VICTIMS

Victim's assistance programs pay for psychological counseling for crime victims in every state. Approximately 10 percent of crime victims request psychological assistance through this program. It may be that potential mental health clients are never informed of this option by law enforcement officials, or others responsible for informing crime victims of this program. Information on use by people with a developmental disability is unknown.

Because so few crime victims access the Victims of Crime Program, its under-use by people with developmental disabilities is likely to continue.

Specialized services for victims with disabilities or generic services that include people with disabilities, are provided by a number of organizations, yet no data exist on either the presence of programs or utilization of rape treatment centers, national advocacy centers, government-sponsored child abuse counseling programs, and government-sponsored domestic violence programs. Vertical prosecution units—in which a single prosecutor handles the case from filing through sentencing hearing—might be enormously supportive to people with disabilities, noted Baladerian, but these are few and far between. Anecdotal evidence from such units suggest they result in an increase in convictions in crimes against people with disabilities.

There are thousands of rape crisis centers and domestic violence shelters across the country, yet very few can accommodate the needs of women with developmental disabilities or mental retardation. This is definitely problematic, since it can be more difficult for women with developmental disabilities to leave abusive relationships and to find and then obtain services.

Project Action is a program of the Seattle Rape Relief, Advocacy and Education that addresses sexual assault among people with disabilities. The mission of Project Action is to challenge the myth that people with disabilities are asexual, incompetent, and dependent. These myths are replaced with information and actions that support the empowerment and rights of people with disabilities. Project services include in-service professional training, case consultation, and resource referral, as well as providing direct services to people who have been victimized. The main focus is currently on providing community education to care providers because of the high demand for such programs. The training programs are presented in group homes and are tailored to the needs of each. Project Action services about 500 to 600 care providers a year across the state of Washington.

ABUSE AWARENESS AND PERSONAL SAFETY PROGRAMS

Baladerian notes that there appear to be few abuse awareness educational programs for people with developmental disabilities. She has found that some members of the advocacy and support community appear to be fearful that discussing crimes will induce untoward fear in the students. Others seem to believe that discussing sexual crimes will lead to sexual interest and thus to sexual activity, and the resultant "problems" this will engender. Many members of the disability advocacy community thus have expressed strong reservations about conducting such educational programs. Some communities have, however, developed personal safety programs with good results.

The Portland, Oregon, Police Department developed a unique personal safety training and police awareness training program for adults with developmental disabilities. Their goal was to help prevent victimization, and if it did occur, to educate the victims about reporting the crime. With funding from the Bureau of Justice Assistance, the Portland police developed the *Safety Zone: Cops Talk* curriculum, which incorporated 27 lesson plans on topics ranging from being safe on the bus to staying away from friends who use drugs and alcohol. The Police Bureau delivered the safety training to nearly 1,000 adults with disabilities and over 300 of their family members. The program evaluation demonstrates that, as a result of classes, students retained knowledge learned, made safer choices that may result in reduced victimization and criminal offending, and have improved relationships with police (the curriculum and evaluation are available at www.teleport.com/~police).

Baladerian concluded that children and adults with developmental disabilities, as well as their parents or care providers, should be provided information about abuse and criminal victimization. The curriculum should be adapted to the particular needs of the community and the audience. It is best if the curriculum includes at minimum: a protocol for planned repeated presentations, pre- and post-testing to evaluate effectiveness of learning, the inclusion of an individualized response plan, feedback from the community and program participants, a measure of effectiveness, and endorsement from local officials.

BARRIERS TO RECEIVING SERVICES

Many agencies, organizations, and even courts are not fully accessible to people with disabilities. These deficiencies should have been repaired by July 1994, which was the deadline for accessibility compliance with the Americans with Disabilities Act (ADA). In addition to the physical site being accessible, under ADA, services, materials, and communication must be available to people with disabilities. In this area as well, compliance is more the exception than the rule.

Many services are, for the most part, not accessible to victims with disabilities, including mental health treatment for the victim or the secondary victim; outreach efforts, such as public education seminars; and written materials for victims of crime who have disabilities. Shelters for battered women with disabilities are few. Many programs to teach risk reduction strategies are too complicated for many with cognitive disabilities and are administered only once. Worse, participation in risk reduction programs may result in a false sense of safety by participants and a conviction by parents that their child now can prevent or manage an attempted assault, when in fact they cannot.

Baladerian noted that barriers to service delivery include lack of knowledge of the problem, lack of interest in the problem, lack of information on resources to gain skills, fear of additional administrative and fiscal responsibility, overwhelming workloads or overworked agencies, and a lack of understanding of the extent and impact of the problem.

She suggested that facilitators of service delivery include free training to become ADA compliant, grants to make physical accessibility changes in the facility, additional finances for adding new populations to the client census, and opportunities to provide unique training and internship programs that offer the agency a way to distinguish itself from the other agencies and thus become a "gatekeeper" referral source.

7

Research Needs: Statement by the Workshop Chair

Joan Petersilia

This workshop represented an opportunity to highlight gaps in the knowledge about criminal victimization of people with developmental disabilities. I will try to summarize the gaps that were raised in the papers presented at the workshop and in the ensuing discussions. As this report makes clear, very little research has been done to date, so that the current state of knowledge on the victimization of individuals with disabilities is seriously inadequate. The areas covered in the workshop papers and discussion could be condensed into three major areas that require research: (1) determining the nature and scope of victimization of those with developmental disabilities; (2) addressing the needs of crime victims with developmental disabilities in the criminal justice system; and (3) developing and evaluating interventions to prevent the victimization of people with developmental disabilities and programs to assist those who are victimized to cope with the effects of victimization.

Research designed to answer the following questions would begin to fill the gaps in the knowledge about crime victims with developmental disabilities:

- **What is the nature and extent of the problem?** What personal, behavioral, and developmental characteristics identify victims and perpetrators? What are the situational contexts? What are the impacts (e.g., physical, psychological) on victims with developmental disabilities or mental retardation?

• **How does the formal criminal justice system respond to victims with developmental disabilities?** What barriers to access and eligibility exist, and how can they be eliminated and system coordination be improved?

• **What lifestyle variables act as risk factors for personal and financial victimization?** Potential risk factors that have been suggested include level and type of employment, transportation, living companions, type and size of residential living, and social activities.

• **How might one "predict" which persons with disabilities, in which settings, are at highest risk of victimization?** This research would have very practical aims: to assist those who provide services to people with disabilities to identify those persons and settings at highest risk, so that prevention and personal safety programs can be better targeted, and again, to understand the barriers in the current formal response system that prevents more effective interagency collaboration in effectively responding to victims with disabilities.

• **What programs reduce the incidence of abuse and violence, and how might they best be implemented, evaluated, and funded?**

Answering these questions would require a series of incremental research projects aimed at developing the required knowledge base. This endeavor would involve research devoted to survey methodology, research on the interaction of victims with developmental disabilities and the criminal justice system, research on treating victims with developmental disabilities, and research on preventing their victimization. I elaborate the needs in each of these areas.

SURVEY METHODOLOGY

First, research on survey methodology is important to answering the questions about the extent and nature of victimization of people with developmental disabilities. As McCleary and Wiebe pointed out in their paper, the following areas require attention:

• **Developing a sample frame.** No sample frame currently used by state or federal agencies adequately covers persons with developmental disabilities. Research could investigate the use of government master lists (SSI, Medicare/Medicaid) as potential sample frames. Until an adequate sample frame can be developed, determining rates of criminal victimization of persons with disabilities will remain problematic.

- **Specifying appropriate victimization items.** Standard victimization items were written for populations of individuals with no disabilities and relate to existing crime categories (for example, UCR Part I crimes). To adequately tap the victimization of persons with developmental disabilities, survey items may need to be revised to represent victimization scenarios typical of victims with disabilities. Crimes against people with disabilities are often complex, for example, involving characteristics of several categories (robbery-assault, for instance), and the minor details of these crimes are often less important (and less obvious to the victim) than the major aspects. Although specifically designed victimization items may be required, items must be roughly comparable to categories of the National Crime Victimization Survey if comparisons to the U.S. population are to be made. For example, research could test various victimization items with people with developmental disabilities and compare the results to those using standard NCVS items.
- **Interview methods.** Standard interview methods may not be appropriate for victims with developmental disabilities. Research on interview methods has been conducted in the domains of health (for example the Epidemiological Catchment Area Study and the National Comorbidity study) and education. Research could test ways of improving proxy respondent interviews and examine alternate methods, such as use of free drawing by the victims with developmental disabilities, and other methods that have been demonstrated to overcome communication barriers.
- **Interviewer training.** A relatively large core of trained interviewers is needed for an effective victimization survey. Developing training will require substantial research. Historically, interviewer training has been an afterthought in victimization surveys, though again, it has been well studied in the health domain. The problems of the research project outlined can be solved only if the problems of training interviewers are integrated into the larger research questions.

INTERACTION WITH THE CRIMINAL JUSTICE SYSTEM

The second research area seeks to answer the questions about how the criminal justice system currently deals with victims with disabilities and how those dealings can improve. The following research suggestions come from the papers by Davis, Dinerstein, and Grattet and Jenness, respectively:

• **Accommodations in law enforcement.** Few research studies have been conducted to confirm which benefits, services, and programs are most effective for those with certain types of disabilities. For example, what community policing ideas work? Are there problem-solving techniques that allow for the introduction of, or use of, accommodations for people with developmental disabilities? What approaches are being tried by police and disability experts to assist victims, and how successful are they?

Another question involves whether police have or can develop the resources to request an advocate who is familiar with the disability when questioning the victim, and whether such an approach improves interview outcomes. Alternatively, would it be more efficient to have specially trained officers who are familiar with developmental disabilities on the police force to assist in such situations? What would be the impact of creating a specialized program that consists of specially trained police, victim assistance staff, attorneys, probation/parole officers, and judges who all have specific training in developmental disabilities? Each of these approaches may be successful, but we cannot know that or determine which approach is best without evaluation research.

• **Accommodations in victim assistance agencies.** Resources that are available to the public as victims of crime may be less available to those with developmental disabilities. The following victim assistance services could be considered when attempting to serve victims with disabilities: counseling, transportation to court, escorts to court, hearing enhancement devices in court, follow-along services to enable victims to understand court scheduling and proceedings, help with arranging medical treatment following victimization, alternative dispute resolution services, and access to individuals in environments such as nursing homes to monitor possible victimization. Researchers can begin to document where and how these types of accommodations are being provided among those with developmental disabilities and how effective they are in assisting those with developmental disabilities: for example, do they result in increased reporting and court appearances?

• **Accommodations in the courtroom.** Research is needed on the ability of people with developmental disabilities to provide testimony in a court of law. What specific accommodations are both legally permissible and most useful in assisting victims with disabilities to be effective witnesses?

• **The use of hate crime legislation.** A number of states have added disability of the victim as a condition that qualifies certain crimes for hate crime status. Research could evaluate the viability of the prosecution of violence against persons with disabilities as a hate crime, and whether special sentencing provisions permitted under most hate crime legislation serve as a deterrent.

PREVENTION AND TREATMENT

The final area of research concerns programs aimed at preventing the victimization of people with disabilities and treating those who experience victimization. The points below come from the papers by Sobsey and Calder, Baladerian, and Sullivan.

- **Mechanisms of victimization.** The list of potential mechanisms that may contribute to the increased risk of abuse for people with developmental disabilities is long. More research is required to determine which of the mechanisms play a significant role and what other factors are important.
- **Evaluation of prevention efforts**. Many advocacy organizations and criminal justice agencies are experimenting with programs to prevent the victimization of persons with disabilities. These efforts often involve training persons with developmental disabilities how to avoid dangerous situations. Evaluations of the effectiveness of such programs in reducing victimization are critical to ensuring the safety of people with developmental disabilities.
- **Development of treatment programs.** Research on the needs of crime victims with developmental disabilities could help inform the development of appropriate treatment programs, which once developed must also be evaluated.

References

Alvarado, D., and E. Pope
1994 Agnews doctors called negligent in patients slaying. *San Jose Mercury News* (September 28):1B.

The Americans with Disabilities Act Hearing
1998 *Hearings before the United States Commission on Civil Rights.* The Americans with Disabilities Act and Law Enforcement (testimony of Sheldon Greenberg).

Ammerman, R.T.
1991 The role of the child in physical abuse: A reappraisal. *Violence and Victims* 6(2):87-101.

Ammerman, R.T., V.B. Van Hasselt, and M. Hersen
1988 Maltreatment of handicapped children: A critical review. *Journal of Family Violence* 3(1):53-72.

Appelbaum, P.S., and T. Grisso
1995 The MacArthur Treatment Competence Study I: Mental illness and competence to consent to treatment. *Law & Human Behavior* 19:105, 109-110.

Arc of the United States
1996 *People with Mental Retardation in the Criminal Justice System: Access to Justice National Resource List.* Arlington, TX: The Arc of the United States.
1998 *Introduction to Mental Retardation.* Report #101-2, September. Arlington, TX: The Arc of the United States.

Augoustinos, M.
1987 Developmental effects of child abuse: Recent findings. *Child Abuse and Neglect* 11:15-27.

Bachman, R., and L.E. Saltzman
1995 Violence Against Women: Estimates from the Re-designed Survey. *Bureau of Justice Statistics Special Report.* Washington, DC: U.S. Department of Justice.

Baladerian, N.
1991 Sexual abuse of people with developmental disabilities. *Sexuality and Disability* 9(4):323-335.
Batshaw, M.
1997 *Children with Disabilities.* Baltimore: Paul H. Brookes Publishing Co.
Becker, H.S.
1965 *The Outsiders.* The Free Press, Homewood, Illinois.
Benedict, M.I., L.M. Wulff, and R.B. White
1992 Current parental stress in maltreating and nonmaltreating families of children with multiple disabilities. *Child Abuse and Neglect* 16:155-163.
Benedict, M.I., R.B. White, L.M. Wulff, and B. Hall
1990 Reported maltreatment in children with multiple disabilities. *Child Abuse and Neglect* 14:207-217.
Berkeley Planning Associates
1997 Priorities for Future Research: Results of Berkeley Planning Associates' Delphi Survey of Disabled Women. Berkeley, CA: Berkeley Planning Associates.
Birrell, R., and J. Birrell
1968 The maltreatment syndrome in children: A hospital survey. *Medical Journal of Australia* 2:1023-1029.
Bonner, B.L., S.M. Crow, and L.D. Hensley
1997 State efforts to identify maltreated children with disabilities: A follow-up study. *Child Maltreatment* 2(1):56-60.
Bradley, K.
1999 *Achieving Equal Justice for People with Developmental Disabilities and Mental Retardation: Victimization Issues and Prototypical Programs.* Unpublished manuscript, University of California at Irvine.
Braddock, D., R. Hemp, S. Parish, and J. Westrich
1998 *The State of the States in Developmental Disabilities.* Washington, DC: American Association on Mental Retardation.
Brookhouser, P.E.
1987 Ensuring the safety of deaf children in residential schools. *Archives of Otolaryngology and Head and Neck Surgery* 97(4):361-368.
Bronfenbrenner, U.
1977 Toward an experimental ecology of human development. *American Psychologist* 32:513-531.
Brown, H., and V. Turk
1994 Sexual abuse in adulthood: Ongoing risks for people with learning disabilities. *Child Abuse Review* 3(1):26-35.
Browning, D.H., and B. Boatman
1977 Incest: Children at risk. *American Journal of Psychiatry* 134(1):69-72.
Bryan, T., R. Pearl, and A. Herzog
1989 Learning disabled adolescents' vulnerability to crime: Attitudes, anxieties, experiences. *Learning Disabilities Research* 5(1):51-60.

Buchanan, A., and J.E. Oliver

1977 Abuse and neglect as a cause of mental retardation: A study of 140 children admitted to subnormality hospitals in Wiltshire. *British Journal of Psychiatry* 131:458-467.

Bureau of Justice Statistics

1999 *Final Recommendations for Disability Questions.* Washington, DC.

1999 *Criminal Victimization 1998, Changes 1997-98 with Trends 1993-98.* Washington, DC: U.S. Department of Justice.

2000 *Criminal Victimization in the United States, 1997.* NCJ-17446, Washington, DC: U.S. Department of Justice.

Burstow, B.

1992 *Radical Feminist Therapy: Working in the Context of Violence.* Newbury Park, CA: Sage.

Chamberlain, A., J. Ruah, A. Passer, M. McGrath, and R. Burkett

1984 Issues in fertility control for mentally retarded female adolescents: Sexual activity, sexual abuse, and contraception. *Pediatrics* 73(4):445-450.

Cincinnati Enquirer

1997 Jury mulls verdict in scalding, by K. Delguzzi. June 11. [Online.] Available: http://enquirer.com/editions/1997/06/11/loc_klein.html.

Coles, W.

1998 *Admissible in Court: Interviewing Witnesses Who Live With Disabilities,* videotape and investigational guide, Hutchinson MacLean Productions, Lethbridge, Alberta. More information on the training, can be obtained at http:.//www.lis.ab.ca/coles/disability.htm

Craven, D.P.

1996 *Female Victims of Violent Crime.* Report No. NCJ-162602. Washington, DC: U.S. Department of Justice.

Crosse, S., K. Elyse, and A. Ratnofsky

1993 *A Report on the Maltreatment of Children with Disabilities.* Washington, DC: National Center on Child Abuse and Neglect, U.S. Department of Health and Human Services.

Curry, M.A., and L. Powers

1999 Findings from the survey of women with disabilities. Presented at Crime Victims with Developmental Disabilities: A Workshop, National Research Council, Irvine CA, October 28-29.

Davies, R.K.

1979 Incest and vulnerable children. *Science News* 116:244-245.

Dawkins, J.L.

1996 Bullying, physical disability and the pediatric patient. *Developmental Medicine in Child Neurology* 38:603-612.

Denno, D.W.

1997 Sexuality, rape, and mental retardation. *University of Illinois Law Review* (Spring):315-434.

Diamond, L.J., and P.K. Jaudes

1983 Child abuse in a cerebral palsy population. *Developmental Medicine and Child Neurology* 25:161-174.

Elkind, P.
1989 *Death Shift: The True Story of Genene Jones and the Texas Baby Murders.* New York: Onyx.
Ellis, J.W.
1992 Decisions by and for people with mental retardation: Balancing considerations of autonomy and protection. *Villanova Law Review* 37:1779-1804.
Elmer, E., and G.S. Gregg
1967 Developmental characteristics of abused children. *Pediatrics* 40(4, Part I):596-602.
Erwin, T.
1999 Intimate and Caregiver Violence Against Women with Disabilities. Unpublished manuscript. School of Social Ecology, University of California, Irvine.
Farrell, G.
1995 Preventing repeat victimization. In *Building a Safer Society,* M. Tonry and D.P. Farrington, eds. Chicago: University of Chicago Press.
Finkelhor, D., L.M. Williams, N. Burns, and M. Kalinowski
1988 Sexual Abuse in Daycare: A National Study. Executive Summary. Durham, NH: Family Research Laboratory, University of New Hampshire.
Flango, C.R.
1988 *State Courts' Jurisdiction and Terminology for Child Abuse and Neglect Cases.* Williamsburg, VA: National Center for State Courts.
Fox, L., S.H. Long, and A. Langlois
1988 Patterns of language comprehension deficit in abused and neglected children. *Journal of Speech and Hearing Disorders* 51:239-244.
Frankland, B.
1996 Analysis of Data from Client Development Evaluation Reports. Memo, State Council on Developmental Disabilities, Sacramento, California.
Frisch, L.E., and F.A. Rhoads
1982 Child abuse and neglect in children referred for learning evaluation. *Journal of Learning Disability* 15(10):538-541.
Fryers, T.
1993 Epidemiological thinking in mental retardation: issues in taxonomy and population frequency. In *International Review of Research in Mental Retardation,* Vol. 19, N.W. Bray, ed. Novato, CA: Academic Therapy Publications.
Gil, D.G.
1970 *Violence against children: Physical child abuse.* Cambridge, MA: Harvard University Press.

Goodman, G., A. Toby, J. Batterman-Faunce, H. Orcutt, T. Sherry, C. Shapiro, and T. Sachsenmaier
1998 Face-to-face confrontation: Effects of closed-circuit technology on children's eyewitness testimony and jurors' decisions. *Law and Human Behavior* 22(2): 165-203.
Grattet, R., V. Jenness, and T. Curry
1998 The homogenization and differentiation of hate crime law in the United States, 1978-1995: Innovation and diffusion in the criminalization of bigotry. *American Sociological Review* 63:286-307.

Harlow, C.W.

1998 *Profile of Jail Inmates, 1996.* Bureau of Justice Statistics Special Report. NCJ164620. Washington, DC: U.S. Department of Justice.

Hard, S.

1986 Sexual Abuse of the Developmentally Disabled: A Case Study. Paper presented to the National Conference of Executives of Associations for Retarded Citizens, Omaha, NE.

Harris, L. and Associates, Inc.

1986 The ICD survey of disabled Americans: Bringing disabled Americans into the mainstream. Conducted for ICD-International Center for the Disabled, in Cooperation with National Council on the Handicapped. New York: International Center for the Disabled.

1998 *1998 Survey of Americans with Disabilities.* [Online]. Available: http://www.nod.org/presssurvey.html (10/12/99).

Hartford Courant

1998 Deadly restraint: A nationwide pattern of death, by E.M. Weiss. October 11. [Online.] Available: http://www.courant.com/news/special/restraint/day1.htm.

Hemenway, D.

1997 Survey research and self-defense gun use: An explanation of extreme overestimates. *Journal of Criminal Law and Criminology* 87:1430-1445.

Hill, N., T. Mehnert, T. Taylor, M. Kagey, S. Leizhenko, et al.

1986 *The ICD Survey of Disabled Americans: Bringing Disabled Americans into the Mainstream.* New York: International Center for the Disabled.

Hough, M.

1987 Offenders' choice of targets: Findings from victim surveys. *Journal of Quantitative Criminology* 3:355-369.

Jacobs, J., and K. Potter

1998 *Hate Crimes: Criminal Law & Identity Politics.* New York: Oxford University Press.

Jaudes, P.K., and L.D. Diamond

1985 The handicapped child and child abuse. *Child Abuse and Neglect* 9:341-347.

Jenness, V.

1999 Managing differences and making legislation: Social movements and the radicalization, sexualization, and gendering of federal hate crime law in the U.S., 1985-1998. *Social Problems* 46(4):548-571.

Jenness, V., and R. Grattet

1996 The criminalization of hate: A comparison of structural and polity influences on the passage of "bias-crime" legislation in the U.S. *Sociological Perspectives* 39:129-154.

2000 *Building the Hate Crime Policy Domain: From Social Movement to Law Enforcement Practice.* New York: Russell Sage Foundation.

Johnson, B., and H. Morse

1968 Injured children and their parents. *Children* 15:147-152.

Kemp, A., B.L. Green, C. Hovanitz, and E.I. Rawlings

1995 Incidence and correlates of posttraumatic stress disorder in battered women. *Journal of Interpersonal Violence* 10(1):43-55.

Knutson, J.F.

1988 Physical and sexual abuse of children. Pp. 32-70 in *Handbook of Pediatric Psychology*, D.K. Routh, ed. New York: Guilford Press.

Knutson, J.F., and H.A. Schartz

1997 Evidence pertaining to physical abuse and neglect of children as parent-child relational diagnoses. In *Diagnostic and Statistical Manual of Mental Disorders, 3rd edition*, T.A. Widiger, A.J. Frances, H.A. Pincus, M. First, and W. Davis, eds. Washington, DC: American Psychiatric Association Press.

Koss, M.P., L.A. Goodman, A. Browne, L.F. Fitzgerald, G.P. Keita, and N.F. Russo

1994 *Male Violence Against Women at Home, at Work, and in the Community.* Washington, DC: American Psychological Association.

Lang, R.A., and R.R. Frenzel

1988 How sex offenders lure children. *Annals of Sex Research* 1(2):303-317.

Lang, R.W., and J.V. Kahn

1986 Teacher estimates of handicapped student crime victimization and delinquency. *Journal of Special Education* 20(3):359-365.

LaPlante, M.M., and D. Carlson

1996 Disability in the United States: Prevalence and Causes, 1992, from the National Health Interview Survey, Disabilities Statistics Report (7). Washington, DC: National Institute on Disability and Rehabilitation Research.

Larsen, K.H.

1992 Annotation: Rape or similar offense based on intercourse with a woman who is allegedly mentally deficient. *A.L.R.* 31(3d):1227.

Laub, J.H.

1990 Patterns of criminal victimization in the United States. Pp. 23-49 in *Victims of Crime: Problems, Policies and Programs*, A.J. Lurigio, W.G. Skogan, and R.C. Davis, eds. Newbury Park, CA: Sage Publications.

Law, J., and J. Conway

1992 Effect of abuse and neglect on the development of children's speech and language. *Developmental Medicine in Child Neurology* 34:943-948.

Lawrence, F.M.

1999 *Punishing Hate: Bias Crimes Under American Law.* Cambridge, MA: Harvard University Press.

Levin, J., and J. McDevitt

1993 *Hate Crime: The Rising Tide of Bigotry and Bloodshed.* New York: Plenum Press.

Lewis, D.O., J.H. Pincus, B. Bard, and E. Richardson

1988 Neuropsychiatric, psychoeducational, and family characteristics of 14 juveniles condemned to death in the United States. *American Journal of Psychiatry* 145(5):584-589.

Lightcap, J.L., J.A. Jurland, and R.L. Burgess

1982 Child abuse: A test of some predictions from evolutionary theory. *Ethology and Sociobiology* 3(2):61-67.

Luckasson, R.

1992 People with mental retardation as victims of crime. In *The Criminal Justice System and Mental Retardation,* R.W. Conley, R. Luckasson, and G.N. Bouthilet, eds. Baltimore, MD: Paul H. Brookes Publishing Co.

1995 Identification of defendants, victims, and witnesses with mental retardation. In *Defendants, Victims, and Witnesses with Mental Retardation: An Instructional Guide for Judges and Judicial Educators*, R. Luckasson and E.E. Vance, eds. Reno, NV: National Judicial College.

Luckasson, R., et al.

1992 *Mental Retardation: Definition, Classification, and Systems of Support*, 9th ed. Washington, DC: American Association on Mental Retardation.

MacNamara, R.D.

1992 *Creating Abuse Free Environments for Children, the Disabled, and the Elderly: Preparing, Supervising, and Managing Caregivers for the Emotional Impact of Their Responsibilities*. Springfield, IL: Charles C Thomas.

Mansell, S., D. Sobsey, and P. Calder

Sexual abuse treatment for persons with developmental disabilities. *Professional Psychology: Research and Practice* 23(5):404-409.

Maxfield, M.G.

1987 Lifestyle and routine activities in the users of crime: empirical studies of victimization, delinquency, and offender decision-making. *Journal of Quantitative Criminology* 3:275-282.

McAfee, J.K., and S.L. Musso

1995 Police training and citizens with mental retardation. *Criminal Justice Review* 20(1):55-65.

McCleary, R., R. Mulnard, and W.R. Shankle

1996a Hysterectomy risk in dementia: Evidence from the 1986 Mortality Followback Survey. *Alzheimer's Research* 2:181-184.

McCleary, R., M.B. Dick, G. Buckwalter, V. Henderson, and W.R. Shankle

1996b Full-information models for multiple psychometric tests: Annualized rates of change in normal aging and dementia. *Alzheimer's Disease and Related Disorders* 10:1-14.

McPherson, C.

1991 Violence as it affects disabled women: A view from Canada. Pp. 54-57 in *Women and Disability*, E. Boylan, ed. London: Zed Books Ltd.

Meier, R.T., and T.D. Miethe

1993 Understanding theories of criminal victimization. In *Crime and Justice: A Review of Research*, Vol. 17, M. Tonry, ed. Chicago, IL: University of Chicago Press.

Mian, M., W. Wehrspann, H. Klajner-Diamond, D. LeBaron, and C. Winder

1986 Review of 125 children six years of age and under who were sexually abused. *Child Abuse and Neglect* 10:223-229.

National Clearinghouse on Family Violence

1998 Family Violence Against Women with Disabilities. *Health Canada Online* [Online]. Available: http://www.hc-sc.ca/hppb/familyviolence/womendiseng.html [10/23/1998].

National Coalition Against Domestic Violence

1996 *Open Minds, Open Doors*. Denver: National Coalition Against Domestic Violence.

Neutra, R., J. Levy, and D. Parker
1977 Cultrual expectations versus reality in Navajo seizure patterns and sick roles. *Culture, Medicine, and Psychiatry* 1:225-275.
Norton, C.
1994 *Disturbed Ground.* New York: Avon Books.
Nosek, M.A., and C.A. Howland
1998 Abuse and Women with Disabilities. *Violence Against Women Online Resources.* [Online]. Available: http://www.vaw.umn.edu/Vawnet/disab.htm. [11/1999].
O'Brien, R.
1985 *Crime and Victimization Data.* Beverly Hills: Sage.
Office for Victims of Crime
1998 *New Directions from the Field: Victims' Rights and Services for the 21st Century.* Washington, DC: U.S. Department of Justice.
Petersilia, J.
1997 Justice for all? Offenders with mental retardation and the California Corrections System. *The Prison Journal* 77(4).
2000a *Doing Justice: Criminal Offenders with Developmental Disabilities.* Berkeley, CA: California Policy Research Center, University of California.
2000b Invisible victims: Violence against persons with developmental disabilities. *Human Rights* 27:9-13.
Phillips, S., and R. Grattet
1999 Judicial rhetoric, meaning-making, and the institutionalization of hate crime law. Unpublished manuscript.
Pillemer, K., and D. Finkelhor
1989 Causes of elder abuse: Caregiver stress versus problem relatives. *American Journal of Orthopsychiatry* 59:179-187.
Portland Police Bureau
1999 *Safety Zone: Cops Talk, Evaluation Summary.* Portland, OR.
Putnam, F.W., J. Guroff, E.X. Silberman, L. Barban, and R.M. Post
1986 The clinical phenomenology of multiple personality disorders: Review of 100 recent cases. *Journal of Clinical Psychiatry* 47(6):285-293.
Rennison, C., and S. Welchans
2000 *Intimate Partner Violence.* Washington, DC: Bureau of Justice Statistics, U.S. Department of Justice.
Roeher Institute
1994 *Violence and People with Disabilities: A Review of the Literature.* Ottawa, Ontario: The Roeher Institute.
Roland, E., and E. Munthe, eds.
1989 *Bullying: An International Perspective.* London, England: David Fulton.
Sanders, A., J. Creaton, S. Bird, and L. Weber
1997 *Victims with Learning Disabilities: Negotiating the Criminal Justice System.* Oxford: Centre for Criminological Research, University of Oxford.
Sangrund, A., R.W. Gaines, and A.H. Green
1974 Child abuse and mental retardation: A problem of cause and effect. *American Journal of Mental Deficiency* 79(3):327-330.

Schilling, R.F., and S.P. Schinke
1984 Maltreatment and mental retardation. Pp. 11-22 in *Perspectives and Progress in Mental Retardation*, J.M. Bern, ed. Baltimore, MD: University Park Press.

Schilling, R.F., M.A. Kirkham, and S.P. Schinke
1986 Do child correction services neglect developmentally disabled children? *Education and Training of the Mentally Retarded* 21:21-26.

Senn, C.Y.
1988 *Vulnerable: Sexual Abuse and People with an Intellectual Handicap.* Downsview, Ontario: G. Allan Roeher Institute.

Shapiro, J.P.
1993 *No Pity: People with Disabilities Forging a New Civil Rights Movement.* New York: Random House.

Singer, P.
1979 *Practical Ethics.* Cambridge: Cambridge University Press.

Sobsey, D.
1994 *Violence and Abuse in the Lives of People with Disabilities.* Baltimore: Paul H. Brookes Publishing Company.

Sobsey, D., and T. Doe
1991 Patterns of sexual abuse and assault. *Journal of Sexuality and Disability* 9(3):243-259.

Sobsey, D., and S. Mansell
1990 The prevention of sexual abuse of people with developmental disabilities. *Developmental Disabilities Bulletin* 18(2):51-66.

Sobsey, D., and C. Varnhagen
1988 *Sexual Abuse, Assault, and Exploitation of People with Disabilities.* Ottawa, Ontario: Health and Welfare Canada.

Sobsey, D., D. Wells, R. Lucardie, and S. Mansell
1995 *Violence & Disability: An Annotated Bibliography.* Baltimore: Brookes Publishing.

Solomons, G.
1979 Child abuse and developmental disabilities. *Developmental Medicine and Child Neurology* 21:101-105.

Soule, S., and J. Earl
1999 "All men are created equal": The differential protection of minority groups in hate crime legislation. Presented at the annual meeting of the American Sociological Association, Chicago, IL.

Souther, M.D.
1986 Developmentally disabled, abused and neglected children. In *Perspectives on Child Maltreatment in the Mid 80s.* Publication No. OHDS 84-30338. Washington, DC: U.S. Department of Health and Human Services.

St. Louis Post-Dispatch
1998 Prosecutor drops case against lieutenant; no police remain charged in retarded man's beating, by T. Bryant. May 7:B1.

Starr, R., K.N. Dietrich, J. Fischhoff, S. Ceresnie, and D. Zweier
1984 The contribution of handicapping conditions to child abuse. *Topics in Early Childhood Special Education* 4(1):55-69.

Stefan, S.
1996 Silencing the different voice: Competence, feminist theory and law. *University of Miami Law Review* 47:763-778.

Strohmer, D., and H. Prout
1994 *Counseling and Psychotherapy with Persons with Mental Retardation and Borderline Intelligence.* Brandon, VT: Clinical Psychology Publishing Co.

Stuart, C.K., and V.W. Stuart
1981 Sexual assault: Disabled perspective. *Sexuality and Disability* 4(4):246-253.

Stylianos, S.
1998 Late sequelae of major trauma in children. *Pediatric Clinics of North America* 45(4):853-859.

Sullivan, P.M., and J.F. Knutson
1998a The association between child maltreatment and disabilities in a hospital-based epidemiological study. *Child Abuse & Neglect* 22(4):271-288.
1998b Maltreatment and behavioral characteristics of deaf and hard-of-hearing youth. *Sexuality and Disability* 16:295-319.
1999a Co-occurring Factors Among Disabled Victims of Maltreatment. Unpublished manuscript. Center for Abused Children with Disabilities, Boys Town National Research Hospital, Omaha, NE.
1999b Maltreatment and Disabilities: A Population-based Epidemiological Study. Unpublished manuscript. Center for Abused Children with Disabilities, Boys Town National Research Hospital, Omaha, NE.

Sullivan, P.M., Vernon, M., and J.M. Scanlan
1987 Sexual abuse of deaf youth. *American Annals of the Deaf* 132(4):256-262.

Sullivan, P.M., P.E. Brookhouser, J.M. Scanlan, J.F. Knutson, and L.E. Schulte
1991 Patterns of physical and sexual abuse of communicatively handicapped children. *Annals of Otology, Rhinology & Laryngology* 100(3):188-194.

Taylor, V., and N. Whittier
1992 Collective identity in social movement communities: Lesbian feminist mobilization. Pp. 104-129 in *Frontiers in Social Movement Theory,* A. Morris and C. McClurg Mueller, eds. New Haven: Yale University Press.

Tjaden, P., and N. Thoennes
2000 *Extent, Nature, and Consequences of Intimate Partner Violence: Findings From the National Violence Against Women Survey.* Washington, DC: National Institute of Justice, U.S. Department of Justice.

Turk, V., and H. Brown
1992 Sexual abuse of adults with learning disabilities. Paper presented at the Conference of the International Association for Scientific Study of Mental Deficiency, Brisbane, Australia.

Tyiska, C.
1998 *OVC Bulletin: Working with Victims of Crime with Disabilities.* NCJ 172838 (September). Washington, DC: U.S. Department of Justice, Office of Justice Programs, Office for Victims of Crime. Available at http://www.ojp/usdoj.gov/ovc/factshts/disbled.txt.

U.S. Census Bureau

1997 Americans with disabilities, 1994-95. John M. McNeil. Household Economic Studies. *Current Population Reports.* P 7061. Washington, DC: U.S. Department of Commerce.

U.S. Department of Health and Human Services

1999 *The AFCARS Report* [Online]. Available at: http://www.acf.dhhs.gov/programs/ch/stats/afcars/rpt0199.htm.

von Hentig, N.

1948 *The Criminal and His Victim.* New Haven, CT: Yale University Press.

Waters, R.L., J. Cressy, and A.H. Adkins

1996 Spinal cord injuries due to violence. *American Rehabilitation* 22(3):10-15.

Waxman, B.F.

1991 Hatred: The unacknowledged dimension in violence against disabled people. *Sexuality and Disability* 9(3):185-199.

Westat, Inc.

1993 *A Report on the Maltreatment of Children With Disabilities.* Washington, DC: National Center on Child Abuse and Neglect.

Westcott, H.

1991 *Abuse of Children and Adults with Disabilities.* London: National Society for Prevention of Cruelty to Children.

Widom, C.S.

1996 *The Cycle of Violence Revisited.* Research Preview. Washington, DC: National Institute of Justice.

Wilhelm, H.H.

1990 Euthanasia program. Pp. 451-454 in *Encyclopedia of the Holocaust,* Vol. 2, E-K, I. Gutman, ed. New York: Macmillan.

Willging, J.P., C.M. Bower, and R.T. Cotton

1992 Physical abuse of children: A retrospective review and an otolaryngology perspective. *Archives of Otolaryngology and Head and Neck Surgery* 118(6):584-590.

Wilson, C., and N. Brewer

1992 The incidence of criminal victimization of individuals with an intellectual disability. *Australian Psychologist* 27(2):114-117.

World Health Organization

2000 ICIDH-2 International Classification of Functioning and Disability. Available in PDF Format on the Internet at http://www.who.int/icidh/

Young, M., M. Nosek, C. Howland, G. Chanpong, and D. Rintala

1997 Prevalence of abuse of women with physical disabilities. *Archives of Physical Medicine and Rehabilitation* Special Issue 78(December):S34-S38.

RESOURCES ON THE INTERNET

Book Publishers

- Paul Brookes Publishing Company: www.pbrookes.com
- Roeher Books: http://indie.ca/roeher

Government

- Administration on Developmental Disabilities: www.acf.dhhs.gov/programs/add/
- Bureau of Justice Statistics: www.ojp.usdoj.gov/bjs/
- Department of Justice Office of Juvenile Justice and Delinquency Prevention: www.childrenwithdisabilities.ncjrs.org
- President's Committee on Mental Retardation (PCMR): www.acf.dhhs.gov/programs/pcmr
- Office for Victims of Crime: www.ojp.usdoj.gov/ovc/

Legal/Law Links

- ABA Commission for Mental and Physical Disabilities Law: www.abanet.org/disabilitiy/
- ADA Document Center: http://janweb.icdi.wvu.edu/kinder/

National Associations

- American Association on Mental Retardation (AAMR): www.aamr.org
- ARC: www.thearc.org
- National Association of Development Disabilities Councils: www.igc.org/NADDC

Nonprofits

- Alternative Justice Canada: www.lis.ab.ca/coles
- Boystown: www.boystown.org (has research program: Center for Abused Children with Disabilities)
- Communities Against Violence Network (CAVNET) www.cavnet.org
- Consortium for Citizens with Disabilities: www.c-c-d.org/
- JPDas Developmental Disabilities Centre (has links to developmental disabilities, violence, and abuse prevention information web sites): www.quasar.ualberta.ca/ddc/links.html
- Mental Retardation/Developmental Disabilities Research Centers: www.aauap.org/MRDDRC.htm
- National Association of Protection and Advocacy Systems (NAPAS): HtmlResAnchor www.protectionandadvocacy.com/
- National Coalition Against Domestic Violence: www.ncadv.org

- National Victim Center: www.nvc.org
- Pacer (Parent Advocacy Coalition for Educational Rights) Center Project: www.pacer.org Focuses on youth with disabilities in the CJS
- Public Interest Law Center of Philadelphia: www.nag4justice.org (National Advisory Group for Justice)

University Links/Institutions

- Baylor College of Medicine, Center for Research on Women with Disabilities: www.bcm.tmc.edu/crowd
- International Coalition on Abuse and Disability: www.quasar.ualberta.ca/ddc/ICAD.html
- SUNY Buffalo (Cornucopia of Disability Information): http://codi.buffalo.edu/
- Temple University Institute on Disabilities: www.temple.edu/inst_disabilities
- UCSF Disabilities Statistics Center: http://dsc.ucsf.edu/default.html
- University Affiliated Programs (UAPs): www.aauap.org/

Other

- Adults with Vulnerability home page: http://library.utoronto.ca/www/aging/awvhome.htm
- Berkeley Planning Associates: www.bpacal.com/ Service needs of women with disabilities
- Pavnet — Partnership against violence network: www.pavnet.org

Appendix

Workshop Materials

AGENDA

October 28-29, 1999

The Lecture Room, Arnold and Mabel Beckman Center
National Academies, 100 Academy Drive, Irvine, California

Thursday, October 28, 1999

8:30-8:45 Welcome
Carol Petrie, Director
Committee on Law and Justice, National Research Council

Nancy Crowell, Study Director
National Research Council

Joan Petersilia, Professor, Criminology, Law & Society
University of California, Irvine, and
Vice Chair, Committee on Law and Justice

8:45-9:00 Introduction — Objectives of Workshop
Joan Petersilia

9:00-10:30 The Nature and Extent of Crimes Against Persons with Developmental Disabilities
Ruth Luckasson, Professor of Special Education
University of New Mexico

Comments

Beverly Frantz, Institute on Disabilities
Temple University

Jody Wildy, Director
Center for Independent Living, Washington, DC

Discussion

10:30-10:45 BREAK

10:45-12:15 Why Are Victims with Disabilities at High Risk for Victimization: Conceptual and Theoretical Issues

Richard Sobsey, Professor
Department of Educational Psychology
University of Alberta, Edmonton

Peter Calder, Professor Emeritus
Department of Educational Psychology
University of Alberta, Edmonton

Comments

Ryan Wright, Deputy District Attorney
Victims Service Unit
Ventura County, CA District Attorney's Office

Valeri Criino-Paez, Victim Advocate
Ventura County, CA District Attorney's Office

Discussion

12:15-12:45	Findings From the Survey of Women with Disabilities Mary Ann Curry, Professor, Oregon Health Services University School of Nursing Laurie Powers Center on Self Determination Oregon Institute on Disability and Development Discussion
12:45-2:00	Lunch Jan Chaiken, Director Bureau of Justice Statistics
2:00-3:30	Measuring the Incidence and Prevalence of Crime Against Persons with Disabilities: Methodological Concerns and Remedies Richard McCleary, Professor School of Social Ecology University of California, Irvine Douglas Wiebe School of Social Ecology University of California, Irvine Comments Colin Loftin, Professor School of Criminal Justice University of Albany Rick Ingraham, Chief, Health and Wellness Section Department of Development Services State of California Discussion

3:30-3:45	Break
3:45-5:15	Abuse and Neglect of Children with Disabilities Patricia M. Sullivan Center for Abused Children with Disabilities Boys Town National Research Hospital Comments John Knutson, Professor Department of Psychology University of Iowa Paul Feuerstein, Executive Director Barrier Free Living, Inc., New York, NY Discussion
5:15-5:30	Wrap-up Joan Petersilia
5:20	Adjourn
5:30	Reception

Friday, October 29, 1999

8:30-8:45	Welcome
8:45-10:15	Mental Retardation and Court Processing: Consent, Capacity, and Other Key Legal Issues Robert D. Dinerstein, Associate Dean for Academic Affairs American University, Washington College of Law Comments

Gail Goodman, Professor
Department of Psychology
University of California, Davis

Susan Stefan, Professor of Law
University of Miami School of Law

Discussion

10:15-10:30 BREAK

10:30-12:00 The Role of Law Enforcement in Providing Effective and ADA-Compliant Service to Victims with Developmental Disabilities

Leigh Ann Davis
The Arc of the United States, Arlington, Texas

Comments

Linda Teplin, Professor
Department of Psychiatry
School of Medicine
Northwestern University

Barry Perrou, Psychologist
Los Angeles County Sheriff's Department

Discussion

12:00-1:30 Lunch

Laura Mosqueda, Director of Geriatrics and Clinical Associate Professor of Family Medicine
UCI College of Medicine

1:30-3:00 Toward Victim Recovery: Meeting the Needs of Crime Victims with Disabilities

Nora J. Baladerian
Spectrum Institute
Culver City, California

Comments

Dean Kilpatrick, Professor
National Crime Victims Research and Treatment Center
Medical University of South Carolina

Lawrence H. Bergmann, President
Post Trauma Resources
Columbia, South Carolina

Discussion

3:15 Break

3:30-5:00 Advocacy, Hate Crime Legislation, and Other Legal Means to Respond to Victims with Disabilities

Ryken Grattet, Associate Professor
Sociology Department
University of California, Davis

Valerie Jenness, Associate Professor
Department of Criminology, Law & Society
University of California, Irvine

Comments

Wayne Logan, Associate Professor
School of Criminal Justice
University of Albany

Marc Dubin, Trial Attorney
Civil Rights Division
Disability Rights Section
U.S. Department of Justice

Discussion

5:00 Wrap-up and adjourn

BACKGROUND PAPERS

Crimes Against Persons with Developmental Disabilities: An Overview
Ruth Luckasson

Violence Against People with Disabilities: A Conceptual Analysis
Richard Sobsey and Peter Calder

Measuring the Victimization Risk of the Developmentally Disabled: Methodological Problems and Solutions
Richard McCleary and Douglas Wiebe

Violence and Abuse Against Children with Disabilities
Patricia M. Sullivan

Participation of People with Mental Retardation in Court Proceedings: Consent, Capacity, and Accommodation
Robert D. Dinerstein

The Criminal Justice Response to Victims with Developmental Disabilities: Utilizing Effective ADA Accommodations
Leigh Ann Davis

Children and Adults with Developmental Disabilities: Maltreatment Update
Nora J. Baladerian

Policy Responses to the Victimization of Persons with Disabilities: An Assessment of the Viability of Using Hate Crime Law to Enhance the Status and Welfare of Persons with Disabilities
Ryken Grattet and Valerie Jenness

BIOGRAPHICAL SKETCHES OF PAPER AUTHORS

Joan Petersilia (*Workshop Chair*) is professor of criminology, law, and society in the School of Social Ecology at the University of California, Irvine. She conducts research on various aspects of crime and public policy, focusing on both methodology and substance. Her research and teaching covers research methods, program evaluation, policy analysis, juvenile delinquency, corrections, and criminology.

Nora Baladerian is a licensed clinical psychologist, licensed marriage and family therapist, certified sex therapist, board certified forensic examiner, and certified substance abuse professional. Since 1972, she has worked in the areas of child abuse and developmental disabilities and the abuse of dependent adults. She is the director of the Disability, Abuse and Personal Rights Project of SPECTRUM Institute in Los Angeles, California, and cochair of the Los Angeles County Child Abuse Council for Children with Disabilities, and the immediate past chair of the National Commission on Abuse of Adults with Disabilities (which has now merged with the National Committee to Prevent Elder Abuse).

Peter Calder is a professor emeritus of educational psychology and clinical director of the J.P. Das Developmental Disabilities Centre at the University of Alberta in Edmonton, Canada. Prior to becoming involved with the Centre and working on issues related to individuals with developmental disabilities, he taught and did research in the areas of counseling and school psychology. He has collaborated with Richard Sobsey in a number of studies relating to issues of individuals with developmental disabilities, including a review commissioned by The Law Commission of Canada on the needs of victims of institutional abuse.

Mary Ann Curry is the Grace Phelps distinguished professor at Oregon Health Sciences University School of Nursing. Her program of research focuses exclusively on issues of violence and abuse against women, including women with disabilities. Current projects include a nursing intervention for abused pregnant women, women's risk factors for being killed by an intimate partner, and the abuse experiences of women with disabilities.

Leigh Ann Davis is project specialist of The Arc of the United States in

Silver Spring, Maryland. In 1994 she directed The Arc's Access to Justice Project and developed the only national resource list of its kind solely devoted to the issue of criminal justice and people with mental retardation. She authored *Understanding Mental Retardation: Training for Law Enforcement*, a training curriculum developed for The Arc's 1,000 state and local chapters to use when educating local police officers about mental retardation. She conducts train-the-trainer workshops throughout the country to facilitate continued education of police and people with disabilities.

Robert Dinerstein is professor of law and associate dean for academic affairs at American University, Washington College of Law, where he has taught since 1983. Prior to coming to the Washington College of Law, he was an attorney for five years at the Department of Justice, Civil Rights Division, Special Litigation Section, where he litigated cases concerning conditions in state mental retardation, mental illness, and juvenile institutions. He is coeditor, with Stan Herr and Joan O'Sullivan, of *A Guide to Consent* (1999).

Ryken Grattet is an assistant professor of sociology at the University of California, Davis. His research and teaching interests are in the fields of deviance, law, and public policy. He is completing a book (with Valerie Jenness) entitled, *Bias Crime Politics and Public Policy: Building a Response to Discriminatory Violence*, to be published in the American Sociological Association's Rose Monograph Series by the Russell Sage Foundation.

Valerie Jennes is an associate professor in the Department of Criminology, Law and Society in the Department of Sociology at the University of California, Irvine. Her research focuses on the links between crime and social control (especially law), gender, and social change (especially social movements). She is the coauthor of *Hate Crime Policy in the U.S.: Building a Response to Discriminatory Violence* (with Ryken Grattet), and *Hate Crimes: New Social Movements and the Politics of Violence* (with Kendal Broad).

Ruth Luckasson is Regents' professor and professor of special education at the University of New Mexico. She is the coordinator of mental retardation training programs, and teaches in the areas of legal rights of people with disabilities, special education law, teaching students with mental retardation, and educational leadership. As a lawyer, she also has a long history of working for the legal rights of people with mental retardation. Appointed in 1988, Professor Luckasson chairs the American Association on Mental Retardation's Committee on Terminology and Classification, the major group charged with defining the disability of mental retardation.

Richard McCleary is professor of social ecology and director of the MR/DD Research Center Biostatistics Core at the University of California, Irvine. During the 1998-99 academic year, he was visiting professor of public health (Epidemiology Division) at the University of Minnesota. His research interests include injury and injury-related fatalities, developmental disabilities of the very young and very old, and the relationship between the two.

Laurie Powers is an associate professor of pediatrics, public health and psychiatry and the co-director of the Oregon Institute on Disability and Development's Center on Self-Determination at the Oregon Health Sciences University. She is the director of research for the Rehabilitation Research and Training Center on Health and Wellness for Persons with Long Term Disabilities. She has extensive experience in abuse and violence against persons with disabilities, health and wellness, and self-determination.

Richard Sobsey is a professor of educational psychology and director of the J.P. Das Developmental Disabilities Centre at the University of Alberta in Edmonton, Canada. He has worked with children and adults with severe and multiple disabilities since 1968 as a registered nurse, a certified teacher, and in a number of other roles and since 1986 has been actively involved in research on violence against people with disabilities and in advocating for reforms to reduce the risk of violence. He is author of *Violence and Abuse in the Lives of People with Disabilities: The End of Silent Acceptance?* and many other books and articles on the topic. His current research is on victims of homicide with developmental disabilities.

Patricia Sullivan directs the Research Program on Abused Children with Disabilities at Boys Town National Research Hospital in Omaha, Nebraska. Her research areas of interest include: (1) the prevalence of maltreatment among children with disabilities; (2) efficacy studies of psychotherapy methods with sexually abused children; (3) factors coexisting with child abuse and neglect, such as domestic violence, parental alcohol and/or drug abuse, and family stress factors; (4) the general characteristics of runaways, including the presence of disabilities among them; (5) long-term psychosocial consequences of maltreatment; and (6) identifying base rates and barriers to accessing managed care health services for children and youth with disabilities.

Douglas Wiebe is a Ph.D. student in social ecology and a research associate in the MR/DD Research Center at the University of California, Irvine. His research focuses on public health and epidemiological approaches to reducing violence and injury. He has published research in the areas of statistical methodology, geographical and temporal patterns of street gang activity, violence among inmates, and the relationship between mental illness and violence.